The play was first performed between the years 414 and 412 B.C.

SCENE

A great and barbaric Temple on a desolate sea-coast.

THE IPHIGENIA IN TAURIS

An altar is visible stained with blood. There are spoils of slain **MEN** hanging from the roof.
IPHIGENIA, in the dress of a Priestess, comes out from the Temple.

IPHIGENIA
Child of the man of torment and of pride
Tantalid Pelops bore a royal bride
On flying steeds from Pisa. Thence did spring
Atreus: from Atreus, linked king with king,
Menelaus, Agamemnon. His am I
And Clytemnestra's child: whom cruelly
At Aulis, where the strait of shifting blue
Frets with quick winds, for Helen's sake he slew,
Or thinks to have slain; such sacrifice he swore
To Artemis on that deep-bosomed shore.
For there Lord Agamemnon, hot with joy
To win for Greece the crown of conquered Troy,
For Menelaus' sake through all distress
Pursuing Helen's vanished loveliness,
Gathered his thousand ships from every coast
Of Hellas: when there fell on that great host
Storms and despair of sailing. Then the King
Sought signs of fire, and Calchas answering

Spake thus: "O Lord of Hellas, from this shore
No ship of thine may move for evermore,
Till Artemis receive in gift of blood
Thy child, Iphigenia. Long hath stood
Thy vow, to pay to Her that bringeth light
Whatever birth most fair by day or night
The year should bring. That year thy queen did bear
A child—whom here I name of all most fair.
See that she die."

So from my mother's side
By lies Odysseus won me, to be bride
In Aulis to Achilles. When I came,
They took me and above the altar flame
Held, and the sword was swinging to the gash,

When, lo, out of their vision in a flash
Artemis rapt me, leaving in my place
A deer to bleed; and on through a great space
Of shining sky upbore and in this town
Of Tauris the Unfriended set me down;
Where o'er a savage people savagely
King Thoas rules. This is her sanctuary
And I her priestess. Therefore, by the rite
Of worship here, wherein she hath delight—
Though fair in naught but name. ... But Artemis
Is near; I speak no further. Mine it is
To consecrate and touch the victim's hair;
Doings of blood unspoken are the care
Of others, where her inmost chambers lie.

Ah me!
But what dark dreams, thou clear and morning sky,
I have to tell thee, can that bring them ease!
Meseemed in sleep, far over distant seas,
I lay in Argos, and about me slept
My maids: and, lo, the level earth was swept
With quaking like the sea. Out, out I fled,
And, turning, saw the cornice overhead
Reel, and the beams and mighty door-trees down
In blocks of ruin round me overthrown.
One single oaken pillar, so I dreamed,
Stood of my father's house; and hair, meseemed,
Waved from its head all brown: and suddenly
A human voice it had, and spoke. And I,
Fulfilling this mine office, built on blood
Of unknown men, before that pillar stood,
And washed him clean for death, mine eyes astream
With weeping.

And this way I read my dream.
Orestes is no more: on him did fall
My cleansing drops.—The pillar of the hall
Must be the man first-born; and they, on whom
My cleansing falls, their way is to the tomb.
Therefore to my dead brother will I pour
Such sacrifice, I on this bitter shore
And he beyond great seas, as still I may,
With all those maids whom Thoas bore away
In war from Greece and gave me for mine own.
But wherefore come they not? I must be gone
And wait them in the temple, where I dwell.

[She goes into the Temple.

VOICE
Did some one cross the pathway? Guard thee well.

ANOTHER VOICE
I am watching. Every side I turn mine eye.

[Enter **ORESTES** and **PYLADES** Their dress shows they are travellers **ORESTES** is shaken and distraught.

ORESTES
How, brother? And is this the sanctuary
At last, for which we sailed from Argolis?

PYLADES
For sure, Orestes. Seest thou not it is?

ORESTES
The altar, too, where Hellene blood is shed.

PYLADES
How like long hair those blood-stains, tawny red!

ORESTES
And spoils of slaughtered men—there by the thatch.

PYLADES
Aye, first-fruits of the harvest, when they catch
Their strangers!—'Tis a place to search with care

[He searches, while **ORESTES** sits.

ORESTES
O God, where hast thou brought me? What new snare
Is this?—I slew my mother; I avenged
My father at thy bidding; I have ranged
A homeless world, hunted by shapes of pain,
And circling trod in mine own steps again.
At last I stood once more before thy throne
And cried thee question, what thing should be done
To end these miseries, wherein I reel
Through Hellas, mad, lashed like a burning wheel;
And thou didst bid me seek ... what land but this
Of Tauri, where thy sister Artemis
Her altar hath, and seize on that divine
Image which fell, men say, into this shrine
From heaven. This I must seize by chance or plot
Or peril—clearer word was uttered not—
And bear to Attic earth. If this be done,
I should have peace from all my malison.

Lo, I have done thy will. I have pierced the seas
Where no Greek man may live.—Ho, Pylades,
Sole sharer of my quest: hast seen it all?

What can we next? Thou seest this circuit wall
Enormous? Must we climb the public stair,
With all men watching? Shall we seek somewhere
Some lock to pick, some secret bolt or bar—
Of all which we know nothing? Where we are,
If one man mark us, if they see us prize
The gate, or think of entrance anywise,
'Tis death.—We still have time to fly for home:
Back to the galley quick, ere worse things come!

PYLADES

To fly we dare not, brother. 'Twere a thing
Not of our custom; and ill work, to bring
God's word to such reviling.—Let us leave
The temple now, and gather in some cave
Where glooms the cool sea ripple. But not where
The ship lies; men might chance to see her there
And tell some chief; then certain were our doom.
But when the fringed eye of Night be come
Then we must dare, by all ways foul or fine,
To thieve that wondrous Image from its shrine.
Ah, see; far up, between each pair of beams
A hollow one might creep through! Danger gleams
Like sunshine to a brave man's eyes, and fear
Of what may be is no help anywhere.

ORESTES

Aye; we have never braved these leagues of way
To falter at the end. See, I obey
Thy words. They are ever wise. Let us go mark
Some cavern, to lie hid till fall of dark.
God will not suffer that bad things be stirred
To mar us now, and bring to naught the word
Himself hath spoke. Aye, and no peril brings
Pardon for turning back to sons of kings.

[They go out towards the shore. After they are gone, enter gradually the **WOMEN OF THE CHORUS.**

CHORUS

Peace! Peace upon all who dwell
By the Sister Rocks that clash in the swell
Of the Friendless Seas.

O Child of Leto, thou,
Dictynna mountain-born,
To the cornice gold-inlaid
To the pillared sanctities,
We come in the cold of morn,
We come with virgin brow,
Pure as our oath was sworn,
Handmaids of thine handmaid

Who holdeth the stainless keys,

From Hellas, that once was ours,
We come before thy gate,
From the land of the western seas,
The horses and the towers,
The wells and the garden trees,
And the seats where our fathers sate.

LEADER
What tidings, ho? With what intent
Hast called me to thy shrine and thee,
O child of him who crossed the sea
To Troy with that great armament,
The thousand prows, the myriad swords?
I come, O child of Atreid Lords.

[**IPHIGENIA**, followed by **ATTENDANTS**, comes from the Temple.

IPHIGENIA
Alas, O maidens mine,
I am filled full of tears:
My heart filled with the beat
Of tears, as of dancing feet,
A lyreless joyless line,
And music meet for the dead.

For a whisper is in mine ears,
By visions borne on the breath
Of the Night that now is fled,
Of a brother gone to death.
Oh sorrow and weeping sore,
For the house that no more is,
For the dead that were kings of yore
And the labour of Argolis!

[She begins the Funeral Rite.

O Spirit, thou unknown,
Who bearest on dark wings
My brother, my one, mine own,
I bear drink-offerings,
And the cup that bringeth ease
Flowing through Earth's deep breast;
Milk of the mountain kine,
The hallowed gleam of wine,
The toil of murmuring bees:
By these shall the dead have rest.
[To an **ATTENDANT**]
The golden goblet let me pour,
And that which Hades thirsteth for.

O branch of Agamemnon's tree
Beneath the earth, as to one dead,
This cup of love I pour to thee.
Oh, pardon, that I may not shed

One lock of hair to wreathe thy tomb,
One tear: so far, so far am I
From what to me and thee was home,
And where in all men's fantasy,
Butchered, O God! I also lie.

CHORUS
Woe; woe: I too with refluent melody,
An echo wild of the dirges of the Asian,
I, thy bond maiden, cry to answer thee:
The music that lieth hid in lamentation,
The song that is heard in the deep hearts of the dead,
That the Lord of dead men 'mid his dancing singeth,
And never joy-cry, never joy it bringeth;
Woe for the house of Kings in desolation,
Woe for the light of the sceptre vanished.

From kings in Argos of old, from joyous kings,
The beginning came:
Then peril swift upon peril, flame on flame:
The dark and wheeling coursers, as wild with wings,
The cry of one betrayed on a drowning shore,
The sun that blanched in heaven, the world that changed—

Evil on evil and none alone!—deranged
By the Golden Lamb and the wrong grown ever more;
Blood following blood, sorrow on sorrow sore!
So come the dead of old, the dead in wrath,
Back on the seed of the high Tantalidae;
Surely the Spirit of Life an evil path
Hath hewed for thee.

IPHIGENIA
From the beginning the Spirit of my life
Was an evil spirit. Alas for my mother's zone,
And the night that bare me! From the beginning
Strife,
As a book to read, Fate gave me for mine own.
They wooed a bride for the strikers down of Troy—
Thy first-born, Mother: was it for this, thy prayer?—
A hind of slaughter to die in a father's snare,
Gift of a sacrifice where none hath joy.

They set me on a royal wane;
Down the long sand they led me on,

A bride new-decked, a bride of bane,
In Aulis to the Nereid's son.
And now estranged for evermore
Beyond the far estranging foam
I watch a flat and herbless shore,
Unloved, unchilded, without home
Or city: never more to meet
For Hera's dance with Argive maids,
Nor round the loom 'mid singing sweet
Make broideries and storied braids,
Of writhing giants overthrown
And clear-eyed Pallas ... All is gone!
Red hands and ever-ringing ears:
The blood of men that friendless die,
The horror of the strangers' cry
Unheard, the horror of their tears.

But now, let even that have rest:
I weep for him in Argos slain,
The brother whom I knew, Ah me,
A babe, a flower; and yet to be—
There on his mother's arms and breast—
The crowned Orestes, lord of men!

LEADER OF THE CHORUS
Stay, yonder from some headland of the sea
There comes—methinks a herdsman, seeking thee.

[Enter a **HERDSMAN**. **IPHIGENIA** is still on her knees.

HERDSMAN
Daughter of Clytemnestra and her king,
Give ear! I bear news of a wondrous thing.

IPHIGENIA
What news, that should so mar my obsequies?

HERDSMAN
A ship hath passed the blue Symplegades,
And here upon our coast two men are thrown,
Young, bold, good slaughter for the altar-stone
Of Artemis!

[She rises.

Make all the speed ye may;
'Tis not too much. The blood-bowl and the spray!

IPHIGENIA
Men of what nation? Doth their habit show?

HERDSMAN
Hellenes for sure, but that is all we know.

IPHIGENIA
No name? No other clue thine ear could seize?

HERDSMAN
We heard one call his comrade "Pylades."

IPHIGENIA
Yes. And the man who spoke—his name was what?

HERDSMAN
None of us heard. I think they spoke it not.

IPHIGENIA
How did ye see them first, how make them fast?

HERDSMAN
Down by the sea, just where the surge is cast ...

IPHIGENIA
The sea? What is the sea to thee and thine?

HERDSMAN
We came to wash our cattle in the brine.

IPHIGENIA
Go back, and tell how they were taken; show
The fashion of it, for I fain would know
All.—'Tis so long a time, and never yet,
Never, hath Greek blood made this altar wet.

HERDSMAN
We had brought our forest cattle where the seas
Break in long tides from the Symplegades.
A bay is there, deep eaten by the surge
And hollowed clear, with cover by the verge
Where purple-fishers camp. These twain were there
When one of mine own men, a forager,
Spied them, and tiptoed whispering back: "God save
Us now! Two things unearthly by the wave
Sitting!" We looked, and one of pious mood
Raised up his hands to heaven and praying stood:
"Son of the white Sea Spirit, high in rule,
Storm-lord Palaemon, Oh, be merciful:
Or sit ye there the warrior twins of Zeus,
Or something loved of Him, from whose great thews
Was-born the Nereids' fifty-fluted choir."

Another, flushed with folly and the fire

Of lawless daring, laughed aloud and swore
'Twas shipwrecked sailors skulking on the shore,
Our rule and custom here being known, to slay
All strangers. And most thought this was the way
To follow, and seek out for Artemis
The blood-gift of our people.

Just at this
One of the strangers started from his seat,
And stood, and upward, downward, with a beat
His head went, and he groaned, and all his arm
Trembled. Then, as a hunter gives alarm,
He shrieked, stark mad and raving: "Pylades,
Dost see her there?—And there—Oh, no one sees!—
A she-dragon of Hell, and all her head
Agape with fanged asps, to bite me dead.
She hath no face, but somewhere from her cloak
Bloweth a wind of fire and bloody smoke:
The wings' beat fans it: in her arms, Ah see!
My mother, dead grey stone, to cast on me
And crush ... Help, help! They crowd on me behind ..."

No shapes at all were there. 'Twas his sick mind
Which turned the herds that lowed and barking hounds
That followed, to some visionary sounds
Of Furies. For ourselves, we did but sit
And watch in silence, wondering if the fit
Would leave him dead. When suddenly out shone
His sword, and like a lion he leaped upon
Our herds, to fight his Furies! Flank and side
He stabbed and smote them, till the foam was dyed
Red at the waves' edge. Marry, when we saw
The cattle hurt and falling, no more law
We gave, but sprang to arms and blew the horn
For help—so strong they looked and nobly born
For thralls like us to meet, that pair unknown.

Well, a throng gathered ere much time was gone;
When suddenly the whirl of madness slips
From off him and he falls, quite weak, his lips
Dropping with foam. When once we saw him fall
So timely, we were at him one and all
To pelt and smite. The other watched us come,
But knelt and wiped those lips all dank with foam
And tended the sick body, while he held
His cloak's good web above him for a shield;
So cool he was to ward off every stone
And all the while care for that stricken one.

Then rose the fallen man, calm now and grave,

Looked, and saw battle bursting like a wave
That bursts, and knew that peril close at hand
Which now is come, and groaned. On every hand
We stood, and stoned and stoned, and ceased not. Aye,
'Twas then we heard that fearful battle-cry:
"Ho, Pylades, 'tis death! But let it be
A gallant death! Draw sword and follow me."

When those two swords came flashing, up the glen
Through the loose rocks we scattered back; but when
One band was flying, down by rocks and trees
Came others pelting: did they turn on these,
Back stole the first upon them, stone on stone.
'Twas past belief: of all those shots not one
Struck home. The goddess kept her fated prey
Perfect. Howbeit, at last we made our way
Right, left and round behind them on the sands,
And rushed, and beat the swords out of their hands,
So tired they scarce could stand. Then to the king
We bore them both, and he, not tarrying,
Sends them to thee, to touch with holy spray—
And then the blood-bowl!

I have heard thee pray,
Priestess, ere now for such a draft as this.
Aye, slay but these two chiefs to Artemis
And Hellas shall have paid thy debt, and know
What blood was spilt in Aulis long ago.

LEADER
I marvel that one mad, whoe'er he be,
Should sail from Hellas to the Friendless Sea.

IPHIGENIA
'Tis well. Let thy hand bring them, and mine own
Shall falter not till here God's will be done.

[Exit **HERDSMAN.**

O suffering heart, not fierce thou wast of old
To shipwrecked men. Nay, pities manifold
Held thee in fancy homeward, lest thy hand
At last should fall on one of thine own land.
But now, for visions that have turned to stone
My heart, to know Orestes sees the sun
No more, a cruel woman waits you here,
Whoe'er ye be, and one without a tear.

'Tis true: I know by mine own evil will:
One long in pain, if things more suffering still
Fall to his hand, will hate them for his own

Torment ... And no great wind hath ever blown,
No ship from God hath passed the Clashing Gate,
To bring me Helen, who hath earned my hate,
And Menelaus, till I mocked their prayers
In this new Aulis, that is mine, not theirs:
Where Greek hands held me lifted, like a beast
For slaughter, and my throat bled. And the priest
My father! ... Not one pang have I forgot.

Ah me, the blind half-prisoned arms I shot
This way and that, to find his beard, his knees,
Groping and wondering: "Father, what are these
For bridal rites? My mother even now
Mid Argive women sings for me, whom thou ...
What dost thou? She sings happy songs, and all
Is dance and sound of piping in the hall;
And here ... Is he a vampyre, is he one
That fattens on the dead, thy Peleus' son—
Whose passion shaken like a torch before
My leaping chariot, lured me to this shore
To wed—"

Ah me! And I had hid my face,
Burning, behind my veil. I would not press
Orestes to my arms ... who now is slain! ...
I would not kiss my sister's lips again,
For shame and fulness of the heart to meet
My bridegroom. All my kisses, all my sweet
Words were stored up and hid: I should come back
So soon to Argos!

And thou, too: alack,
Brother, if dead thou art, from what high things
Thy youth is outcast, and the pride of kings
Fallen!

And this the goddess deemeth good!
If ever mortal hand be dark with blood;
Nay, touch a new-made mother or one slain
In war, her ban is on him. 'Tis a stain
She driveth from her outer walls; and then
Herself doth drink this blood of slaughtered men?
Could ever Leto, she of the great King
Beloved, be mother to so gross a thing?
These tales be lies, false as those feastings wild
Of Tantalus and Gods that tore a child.
This land of murderers to its god hath given
Its own lust; evil dwelleth not in heaven.

[She goes into the temple.

CHORUS

Dark of the sea, dark of the sea,
Gates of the warring water,
One, in the old time, conquered you,
A winged passion that burst the blue,
When the West was shut and the Dawn lay free
To the pain of Inachus' daughter.
But who be these, from where the rushes blow
On pale Eurotas, from pure Dirce's flow,
That turn not neither falter,
Seeking Her land, where no man breaketh bread,
Her without pity, round whose virgin head
Blood on the pillars rusts from long ago,
Blood on the ancient altar.

A flash of the foam, a flash of the foam,
A wave on the oarblade welling,
And out they passed to the heart of the blue:
A chariot shell that the wild winds drew.
Is it for passion of gold they come,
Or pride to make great their dwelling?

For sweet is Hope, yea, to much mortal woe
So sweet that none may turn from it nor go,
Whom once the far voice calleth,
To wander through fierce peoples and the gleam
Of desolate seas, in every heart a dream:
And these she maketh empty die, and, lo,
To that man's hand she falleth.

Through the Clashing Rocks they burst:
They passed by the Cape unsleeping
Of Phineus' sons accurst:
They ran by the star-lit bay
Upon magic surges sweeping,
Where folk on the waves astray
Have seen, through the gleaming grey,
Ring behind ring, men say,
The dance of the old Sea's daughters.

The guiding oar abaft
It rippled and it dinned,
And now the west wind laughed
And now the south-west wind;
And the sail was full in flight,
And they passed by the Island White:

Birds, birds, everywhere,
White as the foam, light as the air;
And ghostly Achilles raceth there,

Far in the Friendless Waters.

Ah, would that Leda's child ...
(So prayeth the priestess maiden)
From Troy, that she beguiled,
Hither were borne, to know
What sin on her soul is laden!
Hair twisted, throat held low,
Head back for the blood to flow,
To die by the sword. ... Ah no!
One hope my soul yet hideth.

A sail, a sail from Greece,
Fearless to cross the sea,
With ransom and with peace
To my sick captivity.
O home, to see thee still,
And the old walls on the hill!

Dreams, dreams, gather to me!
Bear me on wings over the sea;
O joy of the night, to slave and free,
One good thing that abideth!

LEADER
But lo, the twain whom Thoas sends,
Their arms in bondage grasped sore;
Strange offering this, to lay before
The Goddess! Hold your peace, O friends.

Onward, still onward, to this shrine
They lead the first-fruits of the Greek.
'Twas true, the tale he came to speak,
That watcher of the mountain kine.

O holy one, if it afford
Thee joy, what these men bring to thee,
Take thou their sacrifice, which we,
By law of Hellas, hold abhorred.

[Enter **ORESTES** and **PYLADES**, bound, and guarded by **TAURIANS**. Re-enter **IPHIGENIA**

IPHIGENIA
So be it.
My foremost care must be that nothing harms
The temple's holy rule.—Untie their arms.
That which is hallowed may no more be bound.
You, to the shrine within! Let all be found
As the law bids, and as we need this day.

[**ORESTES** and **PYLADES** are set free; some **ATTENDANTS** go into the temple.

Ah me!
What mother then was yours, O strangers, say,
And father? And your sister, if you have
A sister: both at once, so young and brave
To leave her brotherless! Who knows when heaven
May send that fortune? For to none is given
To know the coming nor the end of woe;
So dark is God, and to great darkness go
His paths, by blind chance mazed from our ken.

Whence are ye come, O most unhappy men?
From some far home, methinks, ye have found this shore
And far shall stay from home for evermore.

ORESTES
Why weepest thou, woman, to make worse the smart
Of that which needs must be, whoe'er thou art?
I count it not for gentleness, when one
Who means to slay, seeks first to make undone
By pity that sharp dread. Nor praise I him,
With hope long dead, who sheddeth tears to dim
The pain that grips him close. The evil so
Is doubled into twain. He doth but show
His feeble heart, and, as he must have died,
Dies.—Let ill fortune float upon her tide
And weep no more for us. What way this land
Worships its god we know and understand.

IPHIGENIA
Say first ... which is it men call Pylades?

ORESTES
'Tis this man's name, if that will give thee ease.

IPHIGENIA
From what walled town of Hellas cometh he?

ORESTES
Enough!—How would the knowledge profit thee?

IPHIGENIA
Are ye two brethren of one mother born?

ORESTES
No, not in blood. In love we are brothers sworn.

IPHIGENIA
Thou also hast a name: tell me thereof.

ORESTES

Call me Unfortunate. 'Tis name enough.

IPHIGENIA
I asked not that. Let that with Fortune lie.

ORESTES
Fools cannot laugh at them that nameless die.

IPHIGENIA
Why grudge me this? Hast thou such mighty fame?

ORESTES
My body, if thou wilt, but not my name.

IPHIGENIA
Nor yet the land of Greece where thou wast bred?

ORESTES
What gain to have told it thee, when I am dead?

IPHIGENIA
Nay: why shouldst thou deny so small a grace?

ORESTES
Know then, great Argos was my native place.

IPHIGENIA
Stranger! The truth! ... From Argos art thou come?

ORESTES
Mycenae, once a rich land, was my home.

IPHIGENIA
'Tis banishment that brings thee here—or what?

ORESTES
A kind of banishment, half forced, half sought.

IPHIGENIA
Wouldst thou but tell me all I need of thee!

ORESTES
'Twere not much added to my misery.

IPHIGENIA
From Argos! ... Oh, how sweet to see thee here!

ORESTES
Enjoy it, then. To me 'tis sorry cheer.

IPHIGENIA

Thou knowest the name of Troy? Far doth it flit.

ORESTES
Would God I had not; nay, nor dreamed of it.

IPHIGENIA
Men fable it is fallen beneath the sword?

ORESTES
Fallen it is. Thou hast heard no idle word.

IPHIGENIA
Fallen! At last!—And Helen taken too?

ORESTES
Aye; on an evil day for one I knew.

IPHIGENIA
Where is she? I too have some anger stored ...

ORESTES
In Sparta! Once more happy with her lord!

IPHIGENIA
Oh. hated of all Greece, not only me!

ORESTES
I too have tasted of her wizardry.

IPHIGENIA
And came the armies home, as the tales run?

ORESTES
To answer that were many tales in one.

IPHIGENIA
Oh, give me this hour full! Thou wilt soon die.

ORESTES
Ask, if such longing holds thee. I will try.

IPHIGENIA
A seer called Calchas! Did he ever come ...?

ORESTES
Calchas is dead, as the news went at home.

IPHIGENIA
Good news, ye gods!—Odysseus, what of him?

ORESTES

Not home yet, but still living, as men deem.

IPHIGENIA
Curse him! And may he see his home no more.

ORESTES
Why curse him? All his house is stricken sore.

IPHIGENIA
How hath the Nereid's son, Achilles, sped?

ORESTES
Small help his bridal brought him! He is dead.

IPHIGENIA
A fierce bridal, so the sufferers tell!

ORESTES
Who art thou, questioning of Greece so well?

IPHIGENIA
I was Greek. Evil caught me long ago.

ORESTES
Small wonder, then, thou hast such wish to know.

IPHIGENIA
That war-lord, whom they call so high in bliss...

ORESTES
None such is known to me. What name was his?

IPHIGENIA
They called him Agamemnon, Atreus' son.

ORESTES
I know not. Cease.—My questioning is done.

IPHIGENIA
'Twill be such joy to me! How fares he? Tell!

ORESTES
Dead. And hath wrecked another's life as well.

IPHIGENIA
Dead? By what dreadful fortune? Woe is me!

ORESTES
Why sighst thou? Had he any link with thee?

IPHIGENIA

I did but think of his old joy and pride.

ORESTES
His own wife foully stabbed him, and he died.

IPHIGENIA
O God!
I pity her that slew ... and him that slew.

ORESTES
Now cease thy questions. Add no word thereto.

IPHIGENIA
But one word. Lives she still, that hapless wife?

ORESTES
No. Her own son, her first-born, took her life.

IPHIGENIA
O shipwrecked house! What thought was in his brain?

ORESTES
Justice on her, to avenge his father slain.

IPHIGENIA
Alas!
A bad false duty bravely hath he wrought.

ORESTES
Yet God, for all his duty, helps him not.

IPHIGENIA
And not one branch of Atreus' tree lives on?

ORESTES
Electra lives, unmated and alone.

IPHIGENIA
The child they slaughtered ... is there word of her?

ORESTES
Why, no, save that she died in Aulis there.

IPHIGENIA
Poor child! Poor father, too, who killed and lied!

ORESTES
For a bad woman's worthless sake she died.

IPHIGENIA
The dead king's son, lives he in Argos still?

ORESTES

He lives, now here, now nowhere, bent with ill.

IPHIGENIA

O dreams, light dreams, farewell! Ye too were lies.

ORESTES

Aye; the gods too, whom mortals deem so wise,
Are nothing clearer than some winged dream;
And all their ways, like man's ways, but a stream
Of turmoil. He who cares to suffer least,
Not blind, as fools are blinded, by a priest,
Goes straight... to what death, those who know him know.

LEADER

We too have kinsmen dear, but, being low,
None heedeth, live they still or live they not.

IPHIGENIA [With sudden impulse]

Listen! For I am fallen upon a thought,
Strangers, of some good use to you and me,
Both. And 'tis thus most good things come to be,
When different eyes hold the same for fair.

Stranger, if I can save thee, wilt thou bear
To Argos and the friends who loved my youth
Some word? There is a tablet which, in truth
For me and mine ill works, a prisoner wrote,
Ta'en by the king in war. He knew 'twas not
My will that craved for blood, but One on high
Who holds it righteous her due prey shall die.
And since that day no Greek hath ever come
Whom I could save and send to Argos home
With prayer for help to any friend: but thou,
I think, dost loathe me not; and thou dost know
Mycenae and the names that fill my heart.
Help me! Be saved! Thou also hast thy part,
Sending Completed Page, Please Wait ...

IPHIGENIA

'Tis I. This altar's spell is over me.

ORESTES

A grievous office and unblest, O maid.

IPHIGENIA

What dare I do? The law must be obeyed.

ORESTES

A girl to hold a sword and stab men dead!

IPHIGENIA

I shall but sign the water on thy head.

ORESTES

And who shall strike me, if I needs must ask?

IPHIGENIA

There be within these vaults who know their task.

ORESTES

My grave, when they have finished their desire?

IPHIGENIA

A great gulf of the rock, and holy fire.

ORESTES

Woe's me!
Would that my sister's hand could close mine eyes!

IPHIGENIA

Alas, she dwelleth under distant skies,
Unhappy one, and vain is all thy prayer.
Yet, Oh, them art from Argos: all of care
That can be, I will give and fail thee not.
Rich raiment to thy burial shall be brought,
And oil to cool thy pyre in golden floods,
And sweet that from a thousand mountain buds
The murmuring bee hath garnered, I will throw
To die with thee in fragrance. ...

I must go
And seek the tablet from the Goddess' room
Within.—Oh, do not hate me for my doom!

Watch them, ye servitors, but leave them free.

It may be, past all hoping, it may be,
My word shall sail to Argos, to his hand
Whom most I love. How joyous will he stand
To know, past hope, that here on the world's rim
His dead are living, and cry out for him!

[She goes into the Temple.

CHORUS

Alas, we pity thee; surely we pity thee: **[STROPHE**
Who art given over to the holy water,
The drops that fall deadly as drops of blood.

ORESTES

I weep not, ye Greek maidens: but farewell.

CHORUS

Aye, and rejoice with thee; surely rejoice with thee,
Thou happy rover from the place of slaughter;
Thy foot shall stand again where thy father's
stood.

PYLADES
While he I love must die? 'Tis miserable.

DIVERS WOMEN OF THE CHORUS
A
Alas, the deathward faring of the lost!

B
Woe, woe; thou too shalt move to misery.

C
Which one shall suffer most?

D
My heart is torn by two words evenly,
For thee should I most sorrow, or for thee?

ORESTES
By heaven, is THY thought, Pylades, like mine?

PYLADES
O friend, I cannot speak.—But what is thine?

ORESTES
Who can the damsel be? How Greek her tone
Of question, all of Ilion overthrown,
And how the kings came back, the wizard flame
Of Calchas, and Achilles' mighty name,
And ill-starred Agamemnon. With a keen
Pity she spoke, and asked me of his queen
And children ... The strange woman comes from there
By race, an Argive maid.—What aileth her
With tablets, else, and questionings as though
Her own heart beat with Argos' joy or woe?

PYLADES
Thy speech is quicker, friend, else I had said
The same; though surely all men visited
By ships have heard the fall of the great kings.
But let that be: I think of other things ...

ORESTES

What? If thou hast need of me, let it be said.

PYLADES

I cannot live for shame if thou art dead.
I sailed together with thee; let us die
Together. What a coward slave were I,
Creeping through Argos and from glen to glen
Of wind-torn Phocian hills! And most of men—
For most are bad—will whisper how one day
I left my friend to die and made my way
Home. They will say I watched the sinking breath
Of thy great house and plotted for thy death
To wed thy sister, climb into thy throne...
I dread, I loathe it.—Nay, all ways but one
Are shut. My last breath shall go forth with thine,
Thy bloody sword, thy gulf of fire be mine
Also. I love thee and I dread men's scorn.

ORESTES

Peace from such thoughts! My burden can be borne;
But where one pain sufficeth, double pain
I will not bear. Nay, all that scorn and stain
That fright thee, on mine own head worse would be
If I brought death on him who toiled for me.
It is no bitter thing for such an one
As God will have me be, at last to have done
With living. THOU art happy; thy house lies
At peace with God, unstained in men's eyes;
Mine is all evil fate and evil life ...
Nay, thou once safe, my sister for thy wife—
So we agreed:—in sons of hers and thine
My name will live, nor Agamemnon's line
Be blurred for ever like an evil scroll.
Back! Rule thy land! Let life be in thy soul!
And when thou art come to Hellas, and the plain
Of Argos where the horsemen ride, again—
Give me thy hand!—I charge thee, let there be
Some death-mound and a graven stone for me.
My sister will go weep thereat, and shear
A tress or two. Say how I ended here,
Slain by a maid of Argolis, beside
God's altar, in mine own blood purified.

And fare thee well. I have no friend like thee
For truth and love, O boy that played with me,
And hunted on Greek hills, O thou on whom
Hath lain the hardest burden of my doom!
Farewell. The Prophet and the Lord of Lies
Hath done his worst. Far out from Grecian skies
With craft forethought he driveth me, to die
Where none may mark how ends his prophecy!

I trusted in his word. I gave him all
My heart. I slew my mother at his call;
For which things now he casts me here to die.

PYLADES
Thy tomb shall fail thee not. Thy sister I
Will guard for ever. I, O stricken sore,
Who loved thee living and shall love thee more
Dead. But for all thou standest on the brink,
God's promise hath not yet destroyed thee. Think!
How oft, how oft the darkest hour of ill
Breaks brightest into dawn, if Fate but will!

ORESTES
Enough. Nor god nor man can any more
Aid me. The woman standeth at the door.

[Enter **IPHIGENIA** from the Temple.

IPHIGENIA
Go ye within; and have all things of need
In order set for them that do the deed.
There wait my word.

[**ATTENDANTS** go in.

Ye strangers, here I hold
The many-lettered tablet, fold on fold.
Yet ... one thing still. No man, once unafraid
And safe, remembereth all the vows he made
In fear of death. My heart misgiveth me,
Lest he who bears my tablet, once gone free,
Forget me here and set my charge at naught.

ORESTES
What wouldst thou, then? Thou hast some troubling thought.

IPHIGENIA
His sworn oath let him give, to bear this same
Tablet to Argos, to the friend I name.

ORESTES
And if he give this oath, wilt thou swear too?

IPHIGENIA
What should I swear to do or not to do?

ORESTES
Send him from Tauris safe and free from ill.

IPHIGENIA

I promise. How else could he do my will?

ORESTES
The King will suffer this?

IPHIGENIA
Yes: I can bend
The King, and set upon his ship thy friend.

ORESTES
Choose then what oath is best, and he will swear.

IPHIGENIA [To **PYLADES**, who has come up to her]
Say: "To thy friend this tablet I will bear."

PYLADES [Taking the tablet]
Good. I will bear this tablet to thy friend.

IPHIGENIA
And I save thee beyond this kingdom's end.

PYLADES
What god dost thou invoke to witness this?

IPHIGENIA
Her in whose house I labour, Artemis.

PYLADES
And I the Lord of Heaven, eternal Zeus.

IPHIGENIA
And if thou fail me, or thine oath abuse ...?

PYLADES
May I see home no more. And thou, what then?

IPHIGENIA
May this foot never tread Greek earth again.

PYLADES
But stay: there is one chance we have forgot.

IPHIGENIA
A new oath can be sworn, if this serve not.

PYLADES
In one case set me free. Say I be crossed
With shipwreck, and, with ship and tablet lost
And all I bear, my life be saved alone:
Let not this oath be held a thing undone,
To curse me.

IPHIGENIA
Nay, then, many ways are best
To many ends. The words thou carriest
Enrolled and hid beneath that tablet's rim,
I will repeat to thee, and thou to him
I look for. Safer so. If the scrip sail
Unhurt to Greece, itself will tell my tale
Unaided: if it drown in some wide sea,
Save but thyself, my words are saved with thee.

PYLADES
For thy sake and for mine 'tis fairer so.
Now let me hear his name to whom I go
In Argolis, and how my words should run.

IPHIGENIA [Repeating the words by heart]
Say: "To Orestes, Agamemnon's son
She that was slain in Aulis, dead to Greece
Yet quick, Iphigenia sendeth peace:"

ORESTES
Iphigenia! Where? Back from the dead?

IPHIGENIA
'Tis I. But speak not, lest thou break my thread.—
"Take me to Argos, brother, ere I die,
Back from the Friendless Peoples and the high
Altar of Her whose bloody rites I wreak."

ORESTES [Aside]
Where am I, Pylades? How shall I speak?

IPHIGENIA
"Else one in grief forsaken shall, like shame,
Haunt thee."

PYLADES [Aside]
Orestes!

IPHIGENIA [Overhearing him]
Yes: that is the name.

PYLADES
Ye Gods above!

IPHIGENIA
Why callest thou on God
For words of mine?

PYLADES

'Tis nothing. 'Twas a road
My thoughts had turned. Speak on.—No need for us
To question; we shall hear things marvellous.

IPHIGENIA
Tell him that Artemis my soul did save,
I wot not how, and to the altar gave
A fawn instead; the which my father slew,
Not seeing, deeming that the sword he drew
Struck me. But she had borne me far away
And left me in this land.—I charge thee, say
So much. It all is written on the scroll.

PYLADES
An easy charge thou layest on my soul,
A glad oath on thine own. I wait no more,
But here fulfil the service that I swore.
Orestes, take this tablet which I bear
To thine own hand, thy sister's messenger.

ORESTES
I take it, but I reck not of its scrip
Nor message. Too much joy is at my lip.
Sister! Beloved! Wildered though I be,
My arms believe not, yet they crave for thee.
Now, filled with wonder, give me my delight!

[He goes to embrace her. She stands speechless.

LEADER
Stranger, forbear! No living man hath right
To touch that robe. The Goddess were defiled!

ORESTES
O Sister mine, O my dead father's child,
Agamemnon's child; take me and have no fear,
Beyond all dreams 'tis I thy brother here.

IPHIGENIA
My brother? Thou? ... Peace! Mock at me no more.
Argos is bright with him and Nauplia's shore.

ORESTES
Unhappy one! Thou hast no brother there.

IPHIGENIA
Orestes ... thou? Whom Clytemnestra bare?

ORESTES
To Atreus' firstborn son, thy sire and mine.

IPHIGENIA
Thou sayst it: Oh, give me some proof, some sign!

ORESTES
What sign thou wilt. Ask anything from home.

IPHIGENIA
Nay, thou speak: 'tis from thee the sign should come.

ORESTES
That will I.—First, old tales Electra told.
Thou knowest how Pelops' princes warred of old?

IPHIGENIA
I know: the Golden Lamb that wrought their doom.

ORESTES
Thine own hand wove that story on the loom...

IPHIGENIA
How sweet! Thou movest near old memories.

ORESTES
With a great Sun back beaten in the skies.

IPHIGENIA
Fine linen threads I used. The memories come.

ORESTES
And mother gave thee shrift-water from home
For Aulis ...

IPHIGENIA
I remember. Not so fair
A day did drink that water!

ORESTES
And thine hair
They brought us for thy dying gift, and gave
To mother.

IPHIGENIA
Yes: for record on the grave
I sent it, where this head should never lie.

ORESTES
Another token, seen of mine own eye.
The ancient lance that leapt in Pelops' hand,
To win his bride, the virgin of the land,
And smite Oenomaus, in thy chamber hid ...

IPHIGENIA [Falling into his arms]
Beloved! Oh, no other, for indeed
Beloved art thou! In mine arms at last,
Orestes far away.

ORESTES
And thou in mine, the evil dreaming past,
Back from the dead this day!
Yet through the joy tears, tears and sorrow loud
Are o'er mine eyes and thine eyes, like a cloud.

IPHIGENIA
Is this the babe I knew,
The little babe, light lifted like a bird?
O heart of mine, too blest for any word,
What shall I say or do?
Beyond all wonders, beyond stories heard,
This joy is here and true.

ORESTES
Could we but stay thus joined for evermore!

IPHIGENIA
A joy is mine I may not understand,
Friends, and a fear, lest sudden from my hand
This dream will melt and soar
Up to the fiery skies from whence it came.
O Argos land, O hearth and holy flame
That old Cyclopes lit,
I bless ye that he lives, that he is grown,
A light and strength, my brother and mine own;
I bless your name for it.

ORESTES
One blood we are; so much is well. But Fate,
Sister, hath not yet made us fortunate.

IPHIGENIA
O most unfortunate! Did I not feel,
Whose father, misery-hearted, at my bare
Throat held the steel?

ORESTES
Woe's me! Methinks even now I see thee there.

IPHIGENIA
No love-song of Achilles! Crafty arms
Drew me to that cold sleep,
And tears, blind tears amid the altar psalms
And noise of them that weep—
That was my cleansing!

ORESTES
My heart too doth bleed,
To think our father wrought so dire a deed.

IPHIGENIA
My life hath known no father. Any road
To any end may run,
As god's will drives; else ...

ORESTES
Else, unhappy one,
Thyself had spilt this day thy brother's blood!

IPHIGENIA
Ah God, my cruel deed! ... 'Twas horrible.
'Twas horrible ... O brother! Did my heart
Endure it? ... And things fell
Right by so frail a chance; and here thou art.
Bloody my hand had been,
My heart heavy with sin.
And now, what end cometh?
Shall Chance yet comfort me,
Finding a way for thee
Back from the Friendless Strand,
Back from the place of death—
Ere yet the slayers come
And thy blood sink in the sand—
Home unto Argos, home? ...
Hard heart, so swift to slay,
Is there to life no way? ...

No ship! ... And how by land? ...
A rush of feet
Out to the waste alone.
Nay: 'twere to meet
Death, amid tribes unknown
And trackless ways of the waste ...
Surely the sea were best.
Back by the narrow bar
To the Dark Blue Gate! ...
Ah God, too far, too far! ...
Desolate! Desolate!

What god or man, what unimagined flame,
Can cleave this road where no road is, and bring
To us last wrecks of Agamemnon's name,
Peace from long suffering?

LEADER
Lo, deeds of wonder and beyond surmise,

Not as tales told, but seen of mine own eyes.

PYLADES
Men that have found the arms of those they love
Would fain long linger in the joy thereof.
But we, Orestes, have no respite yet
For tears or tenderness. Let us forget
All but the one word Freedom, calling us
To live, not die by altars barbarous.
Think not of joy in this great hour, nor lose
Fortune's first hold. Not thus do wise men use.

ORESTES
I think that Fortune watcheth o'er our lives,
Surer than we. But well said: he who strives
Will find his gods strive for him equally.

IPHIGENIA
He shall not check us so, nor baffle me
Of this one word. How doth Electra move
Through life? Ye twain are all I have to love.

ORESTES
A wife and happy: this man hath her hand.

IPHIGENIA
And what man's son is he, and of what land?

ORESTES
Son of King Strophios he is called of men.

IPHIGENIA
Whom Atreus' daughter wed?—My kinsman then.

ORESTES
Our cousin, and my true and only friend.

IPHIGENIA
He was not born, when I went to mine end.

ORESTES
No, Strophios had no child for many a year.

IPHIGENIA
I give thee hail, husband of one so dear.

ORESTES
My more than kinsman, saviour in my need!

IPHIGENIA
But mother ... Speak: how did ye dare that deed?

ORESTES

Our father's wrongs ... But let that story be.

IPHIGENIA

And she to slay her king! What cause had she?

ORESTES

Forget her! ... And no tale for thee it is.

IPHIGENIA

So be it.—And thou art Lord of Argolis?

ORESTES

Our uncle rules. I walk an exile's ways.

IPHIGENIA

Doth he so trample on our fallen days?

ORESTES

Nay: there be those that drive me, Shapes of Dread.

IPHIGENIA

Ah!
That frenzy on the shore! 'Tis as they said...

ORESTES

They saw me in mine hour. It needs must be.

IPHIGENIA

'Twas our dead mother's Furies hounding thee!

ORESTES

My mouth is bloody with the curb they ride.

IPHIGENIA

What brought thee here beyond the Friendless Tide?

ORESTES

What leads me everywhere—Apollo's word.

IPHIGENIA

Seeking what end?—Or may the tale be heard?

ORESTES

Nay, I can tell thee all. It needs must be
The whole tale of my days of misery.
When this sore evil that we speak not of
Lit on my hand, this way and that they drove
My body, till the God by diverse paths
Led me to Athens, that the nameless Wraths

Might bring me before judgment. For that land
A pure tribunal hath, where Ares' hand,
Red from an ancient stain, by Zeus was sent
For justice. Thither came I; and there went
God's hate before me, that at first no man
Would give me shelter. Then some few began
To pity, and set out for me aloof
One table. There I sate within their roof,
But without word they signed to me, as one
Apart, unspoken to, unlocked upon,
Lest touch of me should stain their meat and sup.
And every man in measure filled his cup
And gave me mine, and took their joy apart,
While I sat silent; for I had no heart
To upbraid the hosts that fed me. On I wrought
In my deep pain, feigning to mark them not.

And now, men say, mine evil days are made
A rite among them and the cups are laid
Apart for each. The rule abideth still.

Howbeit, when I was come to Ares' Hill
They gave me judgment. On one stone I stood,
On one she that was eldest of the brood
That hunted me so long. And many a word
Touching my mother's death was spoke and heard,
Till Phoebus rose to save me. Even lay
The votes of Death and Life; when, lo, a sway
Of Pallas' arm, and free at last I stood
From that death grapple. But the Shapes of Blood—
Some did accept the judgment, and of grace
Consent to make their house beneath that place
In darkness. Others still consented not,
But clove to me the more, like bloodhounds hot
On the dying; till to Phoebus' house once more
I crept, and cast me starving on the floor
Facing the Holy Place, and made my cry:
"Lord Phoebus, here I am come, and here will die,
Unless thou save me, as thou hast betrayed."
And, lo, from out that dark and golden shade
A voice: "Go, seek the Taurian citadel:
Seize there the carven Artemis that fell
From heaven, and stablish it on Attic soil.
So comes thy freedom."

[**IPHIGENIA** shrinks.

Sister, in this toil
Help us!—If once that image I may win
That day shall end my madness and my sin:
And thou, to Argos o'er the sundering foam

My many-oared barque shall bear thee home.

O sister loved and lost, O pitying face,
Help my great peril; help our father's race.
For lost am I and perished all the powers
Of Pelops, save that heavenly thing be ours!

LEADER
Strange wrath of God hath fallen, like hot rain,
On Tantalus' house: he leadeth them through pain.

IPHIGENIA
Long ere you came my heart hath yearned to be
In Argos, brother, and so near to thee:
But now—thy will is mine. To ease thy pain,
To lift our father's house to peace again,
And hate no more my murderers—aye,'tis good.
Perchance to clean this hand that sought thy blood,
And save my people...

But the goddess' eyes,
How dream we to deceive them? Or what wise
Escape the King, when on his sight shall fall
The blank stone of the empty pedestal? ...
I needs must die ... What better can I do?

And yet, one chance there is: could I but go
Together with the image: couldst thou bear
Both on the leaping seas! The risk were fair.
But how?

Nay, I must wait then and be slain:
Thou shalt walk free in Argolis again,
And all life smile on thee ... Dearest, we need
Nor shrink from that. I shall by mine own deed
Have saved thee. And a man gone from the earth
Is wept for. Women are but little worth.

ORESTES
My mother and then thou? It may not be.
This hand hath blood enough. I stand with thee
One-hearted here, be it for life or death,
And either bear thee, if God favoureth,
With me to Greece and home, or else lie here
Dead at thy side.—But mark me: if thou fear
Lest Artemis be wroth, how can that be?
Hath not her brother's self commanded me
To bear to Greece her image?—Oh, he knew
Her will! He knew that in this land we two
Must meet once more. All that so far hath past
Doth show his work. He will not at the last

Fail. We shall yet see Argos, thou and I.

IPHIGENIA
To steal for thee the image, yet not die
Myself! 'Tis that we need. 'Tis that doth kill
My hope. Else ... Oh, God knows I have the will!

ORESTES
How if we slew your savage king?

IPHIGENIA
Ah, no:
He sheltered me, a stranger.

ORESTES
Even so,
If it bring life for me and thee, the deed
May well be dared.

IPHIGENIA
I could not ... Nay; indeed
I thank thee for thy daring.

ORESTES
Canst thou hide
My body in the shrine?

IPHIGENIA
There to abide
Till nightfall, and escape?

ORESTES
Even so; the night
Is the safe time for robbers, as the light
For just men.

IPHIGENIA
There be sacred watchers there
Who needs must see us.

ORESTES
Gods above! What prayer
Can help us then?

IPHIGENIA
I think I dimly see
One chance.

ORESTES
What chance? Speak out thy fantasy.

IPHIGENIA
On thine affliction I would build my way.

ORESTES
Women have strange devices.

IPHIGENIA
I would say
Thou com'st from Hellas with thy mother's blood
Upon thee.

ORESTES
Use my shame, if any good
Will follow.

IPHIGENIA
Therefore, an offence most high
It were to slay thee to the goddess!

ORESTES
Why?
Though I half guess.

IPHIGENIA
Thy body is unclean.—
Oh, I will fill them with the fear of sin!

ORESTES
What help is that for the Image?

IPHIGENIA
I will crave
To cleanse thee in the breaking of the wave.

ORESTES
That leaves the goddess still inside her shrine,
And'tis for her we sailed.

IPHIGENIA
A touch of thine
Defiled her. She too must be purified.

ORESTES
Where shall it be? Thou knowest where the tide
Sweeps up in a long channel?

IPHIGENIA
Yes! And where
Your ship, I guess, lies moored.

ORESTES

Whose hand will bear—
Should it be thine?—the image from her throne?

IPHIGENIA

No hand of man may touch it save mine own.

ORESTES

And Pylades—what part hath he herein?

IPHIGENIA

The same as thine. He bears the self-same sin.

ORESTES

How wilt thou work the plan—hid from the king
Or known?

IPHIGENIA

To hide it were a hopeless thing..
Oh, I will face him, make him yield to me.

ORESTES

Well, fifty oars lie waiting on the sea.

IPHIGENIA

Aye, there comes thy work, till an end be made.

ORESTES

Good. It needs only that these women aid
Our secret. Do thou speak with them, and find
Words of persuasion. Power is in the mind
Of woman to wake pity.—For the rest,
God knoweth: may it all end for the best!

IPHIGENIA

O women, you my comrades, in your eyes
I look to read my fate. In you it lies,
That either I find peace, or be cast down
To nothing, robbed for ever of mine own—
Brother, and home, and sister pricelessly
Beloved.—Are we not women, you and I,
A broken race, to one another true,
And strong in our shared secrets? Help me through
This strait; keep hid the secret of our flight,
And share our peril! Honour shineth bright
On her whose lips are steadfast ... Heaven above!
Three souls, but one in fortune, one in love,
Thou seest us go—is it to death or home?
If home, then surely, surely, there shall come
Part of our joy to thee. I swear, I swear
To aid thee also home ...

[She goes to one after another, and presently kneels embracing the knees of the **LEADER.**

I make my prayer
By that right hand; to thee, too, by that dear
Cheek; by thy knees; by all that is not here
Of things beloved, by mother, father, child—
Thou hadst a child!—How say ye? Have ye smiled
Or turned from me? For if ye turn away,
I and my brother are lost things this day.

LEADER
Be of good heart, sweet mistress. Only go
To happiness. No child of man shall know
From us thy secret. Hear me, Zeus on high!

IPHIGENIA [Rising]
God bless you for that word, and fill your eye
With light!—

[Turning to **ORESTES** and **PYLADES.**

But now, to work! Go thou, and thou,
In to the deeper shrine. King Thoas now
Should soon be here to question if the price
Be yet paid of the strangers' sacrifice.

[**ORESTES** and **PYLADES** go in.

Thou Holy One, that on the shrouded sand
Of Aulis saved me from a father's hand
Blood-maddened, save me now, and save these twain.
Else shall Apollo's lips, through thy disdain,
Be no more true nor trusted in men's eyes.
Come from the friendless shore, the cruel skies,
Come back: what mak'st thou here, when o'er the sea
A clean and joyous land doth call for thee?

[she follows the men into the temple.]

CHORUS
                                                     [STROPHE 1

Bird of the sea rocks, of the bursting spray,
O halcyon bird,
That wheelest crying, crying, on thy way;
Who knoweth grief can read the tale of thee:
One love long lost, one song for ever heard
And wings that sweep the sea.

Sister, I too beside the sea complain,
A bird that hath no wing.

Oh, for a kind Greek market-place again,
For Artemis that healeth woman's pain; '
Here I stand hungering.
Give me the little hill above the sea,
The palm of Delos fringed delicately,
The young sweet laurel and the olive-tree
Grey-leaved and glimmering;
O Isle of Leto, Isle of pain and love;
The Orbed Water and the spell thereof;
Where still the Swan, minstrel of things to be,
Doth serve the Muse and sing!

[ANTISTROPHE 1

Ah, the old tears, the old and blinding tears
I gave God then,
When my town fell, and noise was in mine ears
Of crashing towers, and forth they guided me
Through spears and lifted oars and angry men
Out to an unknown sea.
They bought my flesh with gold, and sore afraid
I came to this dark East
To serve, in thrall to Agamemnon's maid,
This Huntress Artemis, to whom is paid
The blood of no slain beast;
Yet all is bloody where I dwell, Ah me!
Envying, envying that misery
That through all life hath endured changelessly.
For hard things borne from birth
Make iron of man's heart, and hurt the less.
'Tis change that paineth; and the bitterness
Of life's decay when joy hath ceased to be
That makes dark all the earth.

Behold,   [STROPHE 2
Two score and ten there be
Rowers that row for thee,
And a wild hill air, as if Pan were there,
Shall sound on the Argive sea,
Piping to set thee free.

Or is it the stricken string
Of Apollo's lyre doth sing
Joyously, as he guideth thee
To Athens, the land of spring;
While I wait wearying?

Oh, the wind and the oar,
When the great sail swells before,
With sheets astrain, like a horse on the rein;
And on, through the race and roar,
She feels for the farther shore.

Ah me,   [ANTISTROPHE 2
To rise upon wings and hold
Straight on up the steeps of gold
Where the joyous Sun in fire doth run,
Till the wings should faint and fold
O'er the house that was mine of old:

Or watch where the glade below
With a marriage dance doth glow,
And a child will glide from her mother's side
Out, out, where the dancers flow:
As I did, long ago.

Oh, battles of gold and rare
Raiment and starred hair,
And bright veils crossed amid tresses tossed
In a dusk of dancing air!
O Youth and the days that were!

[Enter **KING THOAS**, with **SOLDIERS**.

THOAS
Where is the warden of this sacred gate,
The Greek woman? Is her work ended yet
With those two strangers? Do their bodies lie
Aflame now in the rock-cleft sanctuary?

LEADER
Here is herself, O King, to give thee word.

[Enter, from the temple, **IPHIGENIA**, carrying the image on high.

THOAS
How, child of Agamemnon! Hast thou stirred
From her eternal base, and to the sun
Bearest in thine own arms, the Holy One?

IPHIGENIA
Back Lord! No step beyond the pillared way.

THOAS
But how? Some rule is broken?

IPHIGENIA
I unsay
That word. Be all unspoken and unwrought!

THOAS
What means this greeting strange? Disclose thy thought.

IPHIGENIA
Unclean the prey was that ye caught, O King.

THOAS
Who showed thee so? Thine own imagining?

IPHIGENIA
The Image stirred and shuddered from its seat.

THOAS
Itself? ... Some shock of earthquake loosened it.

IPHIGENIA
Itself. And the eyes closed one breathing space.

THOAS
But why? For those two men's bloodguiltiness?

IPHIGENIA
That, nothing else. For, Oh, their guilt is sore.

THOAS
They killed some of my herdsmen on the shore?

IPHIGENIA
Their sin was brought from home, not gathered here.

THOAS
What? I must know this.—Make thy story clear.

IPHIGENIA [She puts the image down and moves nearer to **THOAS**]
The men have slain their mother.

THOAS
God! And these
Be Greeks!

IPHIGENIA
They both are hunted out of Greece.

THOAS
For this thou has brought the Image to the sun?

IPHIGENIA
The fire of heaven can cleanse all malison.

THOAS
How didst thou first hear of their deed of shame?

IPHIGENIA
When the Image hid its eyes, I questioned them.

THOAS
Good. Greece hath taught thee many a subtle art.

IPHIGENIA
Ah, they too had sweet words to move my heart.

THOAS
Sweet words? How, did they bring some news of Greece?

IPHIGENIA
Orestes, my one brother, lives in peace.

THOAS
Surely! Good news to make thee spare their lives ...

IPHIGENIA
My father too in Argos lives and thrives.

THOAS
While thou didst think but of the goddess' laws!

IPHIGENIA
Do I not hate all Greeks? Have I not cause?

THOAS
Good cause. But now ... What service should be paid?

IPHIGENIA
The Law of long years needs must be obeyed.

THOAS
To work then, with thy sword and handwashing!

IPHIGENIA
First I must shrive them with some cleansing thing.

THOAS
What? Running water, or the sea's salt spray?

IPHIGENIA
The sea doth wash all the world's ills away.

THOAS
For sure. 'Twill make them cleaner for the knife.

IPHIGENIA
And my hand, too, cleaner for all my life.

THOAS
Well, the waves lap close by the temple floor.

IPHIGENIA
We need a secret place. I must do more.

THOAS
Some rite unseen? 'Tis well. Go where thou wilt.

IPHIGENIA
The Image likewise must be purged of guilt.

THOAS
The stain hath touched it of that mother's blood?

IPHIGENIA
I durst not move it else, from where it stood.

THOAS
How good thy godliness and forethought! Aye,
Small wonder all our people holds thee high.

IPHIGENIA
Dost know then what I fain would have?

THOAS
'Tis thine to speak and it shall be.

IPHIGENIA
Put bondage on the strangers both ...

THOAS
Why bondage? Whither can they flee?

IPHIGENIA
Put not thy faith in any Greek.

THOAS [To **ATTENDANTS**]
Ho, men! Some thongs and fetters, go!

IPHIGENIA
Stay; let them lead the strangers here, outside the shrine ...

THOAS
It shall be so.

IPHIGENIA
And lay dark raiment on their heads ...

THOAS
To veil them, lest the Sun should see.

IPHIGENIA

And lend me some of thine own spears.

THOAS
This company shall go with thee.

IPHIGENIA
Next, send through all the city streets a herald ...

THOAS
Aye; and what to say?

IPHIGENIA
That no man living stir abroad.

THOAS
The stain of blood might cross their way.

IPHIGENIA
Aye, sin like theirs doth spread contagion.

THOAS [To an **ATTENDANT**]
Forth, and publish my command ...

IPHIGENIA
That none stir forth—nor look ...

THOAS
Nor look.—How well thou carest for the land!

IPHIGENIA
For one whom I am bound to love.

THOAS
Indeed, I think thou hat'st me not.

IPHIGENIA
And thou meanwhile, here at the temple, wait, O King, and ...

THOAS
Wait for what?

IPHIGENIA
Purge all the shrine with fire.

THOAS
'Twill all be clean before you come again.

IPHIGENIA
And while the strangers pass thee close, seeking the sea ...

THOAS

What wouldst thou then?

IPHIGENIA
Put darkness on thine eyes.

THOAS
Mine eyes might drink the evil of their crime?

IPHIGENIA
And, should I seem to stay too long ...

THOAS
Too long? How shall I judge the time?

IPHIGENIA
Be not dismayed.

THOAS
Perform thy rite all duly. We have time to spare.

IPHIGENIA
And God but grant this cleansing end as I desire!

THOAS
I join thy prayer.

IPHIGENIA
The door doth open! See, they lead the strangers from the cell within,
And raiment holy and young lambs, whose blood shall shrive the blood of Sin.
And, lo, the light of sacred fires, and things of secret power, arrayed
By mine own hand to cleanse aright the strangers, to cleanse Leto's Maid.

[She takes up the image again.

There passeth here a holy thing: begone, I charge ye, from the road,
O whoso by these sacred gates may dwell, hand-consecrate to God,
What man hath marriage in his heart, what woman goeth great with child,
Begone and tremble from this road: fly swiftly, lest ye be defiled.—

O Queen and Virgin, Leto-born, have pity! Let me cleanse this stain,
And pray to thee where pray I would: a clean house shall be thine again,
And we at last win happiness.—Behold, I speak but as I dare;
The rest ... Oh, God is wise, and thou, my Mistress, thou canst read my prayer.

[The procession passes out, **THOAS** and the **BYSTANDERS** veiled; **ATTENDANTS** in front, then
IPHIGENIA with the Image, then veiled **SOLDIERS**, then **ORESTES** and **PYLADES** bound, the bonds
held by other veiled **SOLDIERS** following them. **THOAS** goes into the Temple.

CHORUS   [STROPHE.
Oh, fair the fruits of Leto blow:
A Virgin, one, with joyous bow,

And one a Lord of flashing locks,
Wise in the harp, Apollo:
She bore them amid Delian rocks,
Hid in a fruited hollow.

But forth she fared from that low reef,
Sea-cradle of her joy and grief.
A crag she knew more near the skies
And lit with wilder water,
That leaps with joy of Dionyse:
There brought she son and daughter.

And there, behold, an ancient Snake,
Wine-eyed, bronze-gleaming in the brake
Of deep-leaved laurel, ruled the dell,
Sent by old Earth from under
Strange caves to guard her oracle—
A thing of fear and wonder.

Thou, Phoebus, still a new-born thing,
Meet in thy mother's arms to lie,
Didst kill the Snake and crown thee king,
In Pytho's land of prophecy:
Thine was the tripod and the chair
Of golden truth; and throned there,
Hard by the streams of Castaly,
Beneath the untrodden portal
Of Earth's mid stone there flows from thee
Wisdom for all things mortal.

[ANTISTROPHE

He slew the Snake; he cast, men say,
Themis, the child of Earth, away
From Pytho and her hallowed stream;
Then Earth, in dark derision,
Brought forth the Peoples of the Dream
And all the tribes of Vision.

And men besought them; and from deep
Confused underworlds of sleep
They showed blind things that erst had been
And are and yet shall follow
So did avenge that old Earth Queen
Her child's wrong on Apollo.

Then swiftly flew that conquering one
To Zeus on high, and round the throne
Twining a small indignant hand,
Prayed him to send redeeming
To Pytho from that troublous band
Sprung from the darks of dreaming.

Zeus laughed to see the babe, I trow,
So swift to claim his golden rite;
He laughed and bowed his head, in vow
To still those voices of the night.
And so from out the eyes of men
That dark dream-truth was lost again;
And Phoebus, throneed where the throng
Prays at the golden portal,
Again doth shed in sunlit song
Hope unto all things mortal.

[Enter a **MESSENGER**, running.

MESSENGER
Ho, watchers of the fane! Ho, altar-guard,
Where is King Thoas gone? Undo the barred
Portals, and call the King! The King I seek.

LEADER
What tidings—if unbidden I may speak?

MESSENGER
The strangers both are gone, and we beguiled,
By some dark plot of Agamemnon's child:
Fled from the land! And on a barque of Greece
They bear the heaven-sent shape of Artemis.

LEADER
Thy tale is past belief.—Go, swiftly on,
And find the King. He is but newly gone.

MESSENGER
Where went he? He must know of what has passed!

LEADER
I know not where he went. But follow fast
And seek him. Thou wilt light on him ere long.

MESSENGER
See there! The treason of a woman's tongue!
Ye all are in the plot, I warrant ye!

LEADER
Thy words are mad! What are the men to me? ...
Go to the palace, go!

MESSENGER [Seeing the great knocker on the temple door]
I will not stir
Till word be come by this good messenger
If Thoas be within these gates or no.—

[Thundering at the door.

Ho, loose the portals! Ye within! What ho!
Open, and tell our master one doth stand
Without here, with strange evil in his hand.

[Enter **THAOS** from the temple.

THOAS
Who dares before this portal consecrate
Make uproar and lewd battering of the gate?
Thy noise hath broke the Altar's ancient peace.

MESSENGER
Ye Gods! They swore to me—and bade me cease
My search—the King was gone. And all the while ...!

THOAS
These women? How? What sought they by such guile?

MESSENGER
Of them hereafter!—Give me first thine ear
For greater things. The virgin minister
That served our altar, she hath fled from this
And stolen the dread Shape of Artemis,
With those two Greeks. The cleansing was a lie.

THOAS
She fled?—What wild hope whispered her to fly?

MESSENGER
The hope to save Orestes. Wonder on!

THOAS
Orestes—how? Not Clytemnestra's son?

MESSENGER
And our pledged altar-offering. 'Tis the same.

THOAS
O marvel beyond marvel! By what name
More rich in wonder can I name thee right?

MESSENGER
Give not thy mind to that. Let ear and sight
Be mine awhile; and when thou hast heard the whole
Devise how best to trap them ere the goal.

THOAS
Aye, tell thy tale. Our Tauric seas stretch far,

Where no man may escape my wand of war.

MESSENGER
Soon as we reached that headland of the sea,
Whereby Orestes' barque lay secretly,
We soldiers holding, by thine own commands,
The chain that bound the strangers, in our hands,
There Agamemnon's daughter made a sign,
Bidding us wait far off, for some divine
And secret fire of cleansing she must make.
We could but do her will. We saw her take
The chain in her own hands and walk behind.
Indeed thy servants bore a troubled mind,
O King, but how do else? So time went by.
Meanwhile to make it seem she wrought some high
Magic, she cried aloud: then came the long
Drone of some strange and necromantic song,
As though she toiled to cleanse that blood; and there
Sat we, that long time, waiting. Till a fear
O'ertook us, that the men might slip their chain
And strike the priestess down and plunge amain
For safety: yet the dread our eyes to fill
With sights unbidden held us, and we still
Sat silent. But at last all spoke as one,
Forbid or not forbid, to hasten on
And find them. On we went, and suddenly,
With oarage poised, like wings upon the sea,
An Argive ship we saw, her fifty men
All benched, and on the shore, with every chain
Cast off, our strangers, standing by the stern!
The prow was held by stay-poles: turn by turn
The anchor-cable rose; some men had strung
Long ropes into a ladder, which they swung
Over the side for those two Greeks to climb.

The plot was open, and we lost no time
But flew to seize the cables and the maid,
And through the stern dragged out the steering-blade,
To spoil her course, and shouted: "Ho, what way
Is this, to sail the seas and steal away
An holy image and its minister?
What man art them, and what man's son, to bear
Our priestess from the land?" And clear thereon
He spoke: "Orestes, Agamemnon's son,
And brother to this maid, whom here in peace
I bear, my long lost sister, back to Greece."

We none the less clung fast to her, and strove
To drag her to thy judgment-seat. Thereof
Came trouble and bruised jaws. For neither they
Nor we had weapons with us. But the way

Hard-beaten fist and heel from those two men
Rained upon ribs and flank—again, again...
To touch was to fall gasping! Aye, they laid
Their mark on all of us, till back we fled
With bleeding crowns, and some with blinded eyes,
Up a rough bank of rock. There on the rise
We found good stones and stood, and fought again.

But archers then came out, and sent a rain
Of arrows from the poop, and drove us back.
And just then—for a wave came, long and black,
And swept them shoreward—lest the priestess' gown
Should feel the sea, Orestes stooping down
Caught her on his left shoulder: then one stride
Out through the sea, the ladder at the side
Was caught, and there amid the benches stood
The maid of Argos and the carven wood
Of heaven, the image of God's daughter high.

And up from the mid galley rose a cry:
"For Greece! For Greece, O children of the shores
Of storm! Give way, and let her feel your oars;
Churn the long waves to foam. The prize is won.
The prize we followed, on and ever on,
Friendless beyond the blue Symplegades."
A roar of glad throats echoed down the breeze
And fifty oars struck, and away she flew.
And while the shelter lasted, she ran true
Full for the harbour-mouth; but ere she well
Reached it, the weather caught her, and the swell
Was strong. Then sudden in her teeth a squall
Drove the sail bellying back. The men withal
Worked with set teeth, kicking against the stream.
But back, still back, striving as in a dream,
She drifted. Then the damsel rose and prayed:
"O Child of Leto, save thy chosen maid
From this dark land to Hellas, and forgive
My theft this day, and let these brave men live.
Dost thou not love thy brother, Holy One?
What marvel if I also love mine own?"

The sailors cried a paean to her prayers,
And set those brown and naked arms of theirs,
Half-mad with strain, quick swinging chime on chime
To the helmsman's shout. But vainly; all the time
Nearer and nearer rockward they were pressed.
One of our men was wading to his breast,
Some others roping a great grappling-hook,
While I sped hot-foot to the town, to look
For thee, my Prince, and tell thee what doth pass.

Come with me, Lord. Bring manacles of brass
And bitter bonds. For now, unless the wave
Fall sudden calm, no mortal power can save
Orestes. There is One that rules the sea
Who grieved for Troy and hates her enemy:
Poseidon's self will give into thine hand
And ours this dog, this troubler of the land—
The priestess, too, who, recking not what blood
Ran red in Aulis, hath betrayed her god!

LEADER
Woe, woe! To fall in these men's hands again,
Mistress, and die, and see thy brother slain!

THOAS
Ho, all ye dwellers of my savage town
Set saddle on your steeds, and gallop down
To watch the heads, and gather what is cast
Alive from this Greek wreck. We shall make fast,
By God's help, the blasphemers.—Send a corps
Out in good boats a furlong from the shore;
So we shall either snare them on the seas
Or ride them down by land, and at our ease
Fling them down gulfs of rock, or pale them high
On stakes in the sun, to feed our birds and die.

Women: you knew this plot. Each one of you
Shall know, before the work I have to do
Is done, what torment is.—Enough. A clear
Task is afoot. I must not linger here.

[While **THOAS** is moving off, his **MEN** shouting and running before and behind him, there comes a sudden blasting light and thunder-roll, and **ATHENA** is seen in the air confronting them.

ATHENA
Ho, whither now, so hot upon the prey,
King Thoas? It is I that bid thee stay,
Athena, child of Zeus. Turn back this flood
Of wrathful men, and get thee temperate blood.
Apollo's word and Fate's ordained path
Have led Orestes here, to escape the wrath
Of Them that Hate. To Argos he must bring
His sister's life, and guide that Holy Thing
Which fell from heaven, in mine own land to dwell.
So shall his pain have rest, and all be well.
Thou hast heard my speech, O King. No death from thee
May share Orestes between rocks and sea:
Poseidon for my love doth make the sore
Waves gentle, and set free his labouring oar.

And thou, O far away—for, far or near

A goddess speaketh and thy heart must hear—
Go on thy ways, Orestes, bearing home
The Image and thy sister. When ye come
To god-built Athens, lo, a land there is
Half hid on Attica's last boundaries,
A little land, hard by Karystus' Rock,
But sacred. It is called by Attic folk
Halae. Build there a temple, and bestow
Therein thine Image, that the world may know
The tale of Tauris and of thee, cast out
From pole to pole of Greece, a blood-hound rout
Of ill thoughts driving thee. So through the whole
Of time to Artemis the Tauropole
Shall men make hymns at Halae. And withal
Give them this law. At each high festival,
A sword, in record of thy death undone,
Shall touch a man's throat, and the red blood run—
One drop, for old religion's sake. In this
Shall live that old red rite of Artemis.
And them, Iphigenia, by the stair
Of Brauron in the rocks, the Key shalt bear
Of Artemis. There shalt thou live and die,
And there have burial. And a gift shall lie
Above thy shrine, fair raiment undefiled
Left upon earth by mothers dead with child.

Ye last, O exiled women, true of heart
And faithful found, ye shall in peace depart,
Each to her home: behold Athena's will.

Orestes, long ago on Ares' Hill
I saved thee, when the votes of Death and Life
Lay equal: and henceforth, when men at strife
So stand, mid equal votes of Life and Death,
My law shall hold that Mercy conquereth.
Begone. Lead forth thy sister from this shore
In peace; and thou, Thoas, be wroth no more.

THOAS
Most high Athena, he who bows not low
His head to God's word spoken, I scarce know
How such an one doth live. Orestes hath
Fled with mine Image hence ... I bear no wrath.
Nor yet against his sister. There is naught,
Methinks, of honour in a battle fought
'Gainst gods. The strength is theirs. Let those two fare
Forth to thy land and plant mine Image there.
I wish them well.

These bondwomen no less
I will send free to Greece and happiness,

And stay my galleys' oars, and bid this brand
Be sheathed again, Goddess, at thy command.

ATHENA
'Tis well, O King. For that which needs must be
Holdeth the high gods as it holdeth thee.

Winds of the north, O winds that laugh and run,
Bear now to Athens Agamemnon's son:
Myself am with you, o'er long leagues of foam
Guiding my sister's hallowed Image home.

[She floats away.

CHORUS
SOME WOMEN
Go forth in bliss, O ye whose lot
God shieldeth, that ye perish not!

OTHERS
O great in our dull world of clay,
And great in heaven's undying gleam,
Pallas, thy bidding we obey:
And bless thee, for mine ears have heard
The joy and wonder of a word
Beyond my dream, beyond my dream.

Iphigenia In Taurius by Euripedes

Translated from the Greek by Theodore Alois Buckley

Index of Contents

THE PERSONS
IPHIGENIA.
ORESTES.
PYLADES.
HERDSMAN.
THOAS.
MESSENGER.
MINERVA.
CHORUS OF GRECIAN CAPTIVE WOMEN.

Orestes, coming into Tauri in Scythia, in company with Pylades, had been commanded to bear away the image of Diana, after which he was to meet with a respite from the avenging Erinnyes of his mother. His sister Iphigenia, who had been carried away by Diana from Aulis, when on the point of being sacrificed by her father, chances to be expiating a dream that led her to suppose Orestes dead, when a herdsman announces to her the arrival and detection of two strangers, whom she is bound by her office to sacrifice to Diana. On meeting, a mutual discovery takes place, and they plot their escape. Iphigenia imposes on the superstitious fears of Thoas, and, removing them to the sea-coast, they are on the point of making their escape together, when they are surprised, and subsequently detained and driven back by stress of weather. Thoas is about to pursue them, when Minerva appears, and restrains him from doing so, at the same time procuring liberty of return for the Grecian captives who form the chorus.

IPHIGENIA

Pelops, the son of Tantalus, setting out to Pisa with his swift steeds, weds the daughter of Œnomaus, from whom sprang Atreus; and from Atreus his sons, Menelaus and Agamemnon, from which latter I was born, Iphigenia, child of Clytæmnestra, daughter of Tyndarus, whom my father, as he imagined, sacrificed to Diana on account of Helen, near the eddies, which Euripus continually whirls to and fro, upturning the dark blue sea with frequent blasts, in the famed recesses of Aulis. For here indeed king Agamemnon drew together a Grecian armament of a thousand ships, desiring that the Greeks might take the glorious prize of victory over Troy, and avenge the outraged nuptials of Helen, for the gratification of Menelaus. But, there being great difficulty of sailing, and meeting with no winds, he came to the consideration of the omens of burnt sacrifices, and Calchas speaks thus. O thou who rulest over this Grecian expedition, Agamemnon, thou wilt not lead forth thy ships from the ports of this land, before Diana shall receive thy daughter Iphigenia as a victim; for thou didst vow to sacrifice to the light-bearing Goddess whatsoever the year should bring forth most beautiful. Now your wife Clytæmnestra has brought forth a daughter in your house, referring to me the title of the most beautiful, whom thou must needs sacrifice. And so, by the arts of Ulysses, they drew me from my mother under pretense of being wedded to Achilles. But I wretched coming to Aulis, being seized and raised aloft above the pyre, would have been slain by the sword; but Diana, giving to the Greeks a stag in my stead, stole me away, and, sending me through the clear ether, she settled me in this land of the Tauri, where barbarian Thoas rules the land, o'er barbarians, Thoas, who guiding his foot swift as the pinion, has arrived at this epithet of Thoas, i.e. the swift on account of his fleetness of foot. And she places me in this house as priestess, since which time the Goddess Diana is wont to be pleased with such rites as these, the name of which alone is fair. But, for the rest, I am silent, fearing the Goddess. For I sacrifice even as before was the custom in the city, whatever Grecian man comes to this land. I crop the hair, indeed, but the slaying that may not be told is the care of others within these shrines. But the new visions which the past night hath brought with it, I will tell to the sky, if indeed this be any remedy. I seemed in my sleep, removed from this land, to be dwelling in Argos, and to slumber in my virgin chamber, but the surface of the earth appeared to be shaken with a movement, and I fled, and standing without beheld the coping of the house giving way, and all the roof falling stricken to the ground from the high supports. And one pillar alone, as it seemed to me, was left of my ancestral house, and from its capital it seemed to stream down yellow locks, and to receive a human voice, and I, cherishing this man-slaying office which I hold, weeping began to besprinkle it, as though about to be slain. But I thus interpret my dream. Orestes is dead, whose rites I was beginning. For male children are the pillars of the house, and those whom my lustral waters sprinkle die. Nor yet can I connect the dream with my friends, for Strophius had no son, when I was to have died. Now, therefore, I being present, will to my absent brother offer the rites of the dead—for this I can do—in company with the attendants whom the king gave to me, Grecian women. But from some cause they are not yet present. I will go within the home wherein I dwell, these shrines of the Goddess.

ORESTES
Look out! Watch, lest there be any mortal in the way.

PYLADES
I am looking out, and keeping watch, turning my eyes every where.

ORESTES
Pylades, does it seem to you that this is the temple of the Goddess, whither we have directed our ship through the seas from Argos?

PYLADES
It does, Orestes, and must seem the same to thee.

ORESTES
And the altar where Grecian blood is shed?

PYLADES
At least it has its pinnacles tawny with blood.

ORESTES
And under the pinnacles themselves do you behold the spoils?

PYLADES
The spoils, forsooth, of slain strangers.

ORESTES
But it behooves one, turning one's eye around, to keep a careful watch. O Phœbus, wherefore hast thou again led me into this snare by your prophecies, when I had avenged the blood of my father by slaying my mother? But by successive attacks of the Furies was I driven an exile, an outcast from the land, and fulfilled many diverse bending courses. But coming to thy oracle I required of thee how I might arrive at an end of the madness that drove me on, and of my toils which I had labored through, wandering over Greece. But thou didst answer that I must come to the confines of the Tauric territory, where thy sister Diana possesses altars, and must take the image of the Goddess, which they here say fell from heaven into these shrines; and that taking it either by stratagem or by some stroke of fortune, having gone through the risk, I should give it to the land of the Athenians—but no further directions were given—and that having done this, I should have a respite from my toils. But I am come hither, persuaded by thy words, to an unknown and inhospitable land. I ask you, then, Pylades, for you are a sharer with me in this toil, what shall we do? For thou beholdest the lofty battlements of the walls. Shall we proceed to the scaling of the walls? How then should we escape notice if we did so? Or shall we open the brass-wrought fastenings of the bolts? of which things we know nothing. But if we are caught opening the gates and contriving an entrance, we shall die. But before we die, let us flee to the temple, whither we lately sailed.

PYLADES

To fly is unendurable, nor are we accustomed to do so, and we must not make light of the oracle of the God. But quitting the temple, let us hide our bodies in the caves, which the dark sea splashes with its waters, far away from the city, lest any one beholding the bark, inform the rulers, and we be straightway seized by force. But when the eye of dim night shall come, we must venture, bring all devices to bear, to seize the sculptured image from the temple. But observe the eaves of the roof, where there is an empty space between the triglyphs in which you may let yourself down. For good men dare encounter toils, but the cowardly are of no account any where. We have not indeed come a long distance with our oars, so as to return again from the goal.

ORESTES

But one must follow your advice, for you speak well. We must go whithersoever in this land we can conceal our bodies, and lie hid. For the will of the God will not be the cause of his oracle falling useless. We must venture; for no toil has an excuse for young men.

[**ORESTES** and **PYLADES** retire aside .

CHORUS

Keep silence, O ye that inhabit the twain rocks of the Euxine that face each other. O Dictynna, mountain daughter of Latona, to thy court, the gold-decked pinnacles of temples with fine columns, I, servant to the hallowed guardian of the key, conduct my pious virgin foot, changing for my present habitation the towers and walls of Greece with its noble steeds, and Europe with its fields abounding in trees, the dwelling of my ancestral home. I am come. What new matter? What anxious care hast thou? Wherefore hast thou led me, led me to the shrines, O daughter of him who came to the walls of Troy with the glorious fleet, with thousand sail, ten thousand spears of the renowned Atrides?

IPHIGENIA

O attendants mine, in what moans of bitter lamentation do I dwell, in the songs of a songless strain unfit for the lyre, alas! alas! in funereal griefs for the ills which befall me, bemoaning my brother, what a vision have I seen in the night whose darkness has passed away! I am undone, undone. No more is my father's house, ah me! no more is our race. Alas! alas! for the toils in Argos! Alas! thou deity, who hast now robbed me of my only brother, sending him to Hades, to whom I am about to pour forth on the earth's surface these libations and this bowl for the departed, and streams from the mountain heifer, and the wine draughts of Bacchus, and the work of the swarthy bees, which are the wonted peace-offerings to the departed. O germ of Agamemnon beneath the earth, to thee as dead do I send these offerings. And do thou receive them, for not before thine own tomb do I offer my auburn locks, my tears. For far away am I journeyed from thy country and mine, where, as opinion goes, I wretched lie slaughtered.

CHORUS

A respondent strain and an Asiatic hymn of barbarian wailing will I peal forth to thee, my mistress, the song of mourning which, delighting the dead, Hades hymns in measure apart from Pæans. Alas! the light of the sceptre in the Atrides' house is faded away. Alas! alas for my ancestral home! And what government of prosperous kings will there be in Argos? And labor upon labor comes on with his winged mares driven around. But the sun, changing from its proper place, laid aside its eye of light. And upon other houses woe has come, because of the golden lamb, murder upon murder, and pang upon pang, whence the avenging Fury of those sons slain of old comes upon the houses of the sons of Tantalus, and some deity hastens unkindly things against thee.

IPHIGENIA

From the beginning the demon of my mother's zone was hostile to me, and from that night in which the Fates hastened the pangs of childbirth whom, the first-born germ the wretched daughter of Leda, (Clytæmnestra,) wooed from among the Greeks brought forth, and trained up as a victim to a father's sin, a joyless sacrifice, a votive offering. But in a horse-chariot they brought me to the sands of Aulis, a bride, alas! unhappy bride to the son of Nereus' daughter, alas! And now a stranger I dwell in an unpleasant home on the inhospitable sea, unwedded, childless, without city, without a friend, not chanting Juno in Argos, nor in the sweetly humming loom adorning with the shuttle the image of Athenian Pallas and of the Titans, but imbruing altars with the shed blood of strangers, a pest unsuited to the harp, of strangers sighing forth a piteous cry, and shedding a piteous tear. And now indeed forgetfulness of these matters comes upon me, but now I mourn my brother dead in Argos, whom I left yet an infant at the breast, yet young, yet a germ in his mother's arms and on her bosom, Orestes the future holder of the sceptre in Argos.

CHORUS
But hither comes a herdsman, leaving the sea-coast, about to tell thee some new thing.

HERDSMAN
Daughter of Agamemnon and child of Clytæmnestra, hear thou from me a new announcement.

IPHIGENIA
And what is there astonishing in the present report?

HERDSMAN
Two youths are come into this land, to the dark-blue Symplegades, fleeing into a ship, a grateful sacrifice and offering to Diana. But you can not use too much haste in making ready the lustral waters and the consecrations.

IPHIGENIA
Of what country? of what land do the strangers bear the name?

HERDSMAN
Greeks, this one thing I know, and nothing further.

IPHIGENIA
Hast thou not heard the name of the strangers, so as to tell it?

HERDSMAN
One of them was styled Pylades by the other.

IPHIGENIA
But what was the name of the yoke-fellow of this stranger?

HERDSMAN
No one knows this. For we heard it not.

IPHIGENIA
But how saw ye them, and chanced to take them?

HERDSMAN
Upon the furthest breakers of the inhospitable sea.

IPHIGENIA

And what had herdsmen to do with the sea?

HERDSMAN

We came to lave our steers in the dew of the sea.

IPHIGENIA

Go back again to this point—how did ye catch them, and by what means, for I would fain know this? For they are come after a long season, nor has the altar of the Goddess yet been crimsoned with Grecian blood.

HERDSMAN

After we woodland herdsmen had brought our cattle down to the sea that flows between the Symplegades, there is a certain hollow cave, broken by the frequent lashing of the waves, a retreat for those who hunt for the purple fish. Here some herdsman among us beheld two youths, and he retired back, piloting his step on tiptoe, and said: See ye not? these who sit here are some divine powers. And one of us, being religiously given, uplifted his hand, and addressed them, as he beheld: O son of Leucothea, guardian of ships, Palæmon our lord, be propitious to us, whether indeed ye be the twin sons of Jove (Castor and Pollux) who sit upon our shores, or the image of Nereus, who begot the noble chorus of the fifty Nereids. But another vain one, bold in his lawlessness, scoffed at these prayers, and said that they were shipwrecked seamen who sat upon the cleft through fear of the law, hearing that we here sacrifice strangers. And to most of us he seemed to speak well, and we resolved to hunt for the accustomed victims for the Goddess. But meanwhile one of the strangers leaving the rock, stood still, and shook his head up and down, and groaned, with his very fingers quaking, wandering with ravings, and shouts with voice like that of hunter, "Pylades, dost thou behold this? Dost not behold this snake of Hades, how she would fain slay me, armed against me with horrid vipers? And she breathing from beneath her garments fire and slaughter, rows with her wings, bearing my mother in her arms, that she may cast upon me this rocky mass. Alas! she will slay me. Whither shall I fly?" And one beheld not the same form of countenance, but he uttered in turn the bellowings of calves and howls of dogs, which imitations of wild beasts they say the Furies utter. But we flinching, as though about to die, sat mute; and he drawing a sword with his hand, rushing among the calves, lion-like, strikes them on the flank with the steel, driving it into their sides, fancying that he was thus avenging himself on the Fury Goddesses, till that a gory foam was dashed up from the sea. Meanwhile, each one of us, as he beheld the herds being slain and ravaged, armed himself, and inflating the conch shells and assembling the inhabitants—for we thought that herdsmen were weak to fight against well-trained and youthful strangers. And a large number of us was assembled in a short time. But the stranger, released from the attack of madness, drops down, with his beard befouled with foam. But when we saw him fallen opportunely for us, each man did his part, with stones, with blows. But the other of the strangers wiped away the foam, and tended his mouth, and spread over him the well-woven texture of his garments, guarding well the coming wounds, and aiding his friend with tender offices. But when the stranger returning to his senses leaped up, he perceived that a hostile tempest and present calamity was close upon them, and he groaned aloud. But we ceased not hurling rocks, each standing in a different place. But then indeed we heard a dread exhortation, "Pylades, we shall die, but that we die most gloriously! Follow me, drawing thy sword in hand." But when we saw the twain swords of the enemy brandished, in flight we filled the woods about the crag. But if one fled, others pressing on pelted them; and if they drove these away, again the party who had just yielded aimed at them with rocks. But it was incredible, for out of innumerable hands no one succeeded in hitting these victims to the Goddess. And we with difficulty, I will not say overcome them by force, but taking them in a circle, beat their swords out of their hands with stones, and they dropped their knees to earth overcome with toil. And we brought them to the king of this land, but he, when he beheld them, sent them as quickly as possible to thee for lustral waters and sacrifice. But do thou, O virgin, wish that such strangers may be here as victims, and if thou slayest these strangers, Hellas will atone for thy intended murder, paying the penalty of the sacrifice at Aulis.

CHORUS
Thou hast told wondrous things concerning him who has appeared, whosoever he be that has come to the inhospitable sea from the Grecian earth.

IPHIGENIA
Be it so. Do thou go and bring the strangers, but I will take care respecting the matters here. O hapless heart, that once wast mild and full of pity toward strangers, awarding the tear to those of thine own land, when thou didst receive Grecian men into thine hands. But now, because of the dreams by which I am driven wild, thinking that Orestes no longer beholds the sun, ye will find me ill disposed, whoever ye be that come. For this is true, I perceive it, my friends, for the unhappy who themselves fare ill have no good feelings toward those more fortunate. But neither has any wind sent by Jove ever come hither, nor ship, which could have brought hither Helen, who destroyed me, and Menelaus, in order that I might be avenged on them, placing an Aulis here to the account of the one there, where the sons of Danaus seized, and would have slain me like as a calf, and the father who begat me was the priest. Ah me! for I can not forget the ills of that time, how oft I stretched out my hands to his beard, and hanging on the knees of him who gave me life, spake words like these: "O father, basely am I, basely am I wedded at thine hands. But my mother, while thou art slaying me, and her Argive ladies are hymning my wedding with their nuptial songs, and all the house resounds with the flute, while I perish by thy hands. Hades in truth was Achilles, not the son of Peleus, whom thou didst name as my husband, and in the chariot didst pilot me by craft unto a bloody wedding." But I, casting mine eye through my slender woven veil, neither took up with mine hands my brother who is now dead, nor joined my lips to my sister's, through modesty, as departing to the home of Peleus; and many a salutation I deferred, as though about to come again to Argos. Oh wretched one, if thou hast died! from what glorious state, Orestes, and from how envied a sire's fortune art thou fallen! But I reproach the devices of the Goddess, who, if any one work the death of a man, or touch with hands a woman newly delivered, or a corpse, restrains him from her altars, as deeming him impure, but yet herself takes pleasure in man-slaying sacrifices. It can not be that the consort of Jove, Latona, hath brought forth so much ignorance. I even disbelieve the banquets of Tantalus set before the Gods, as that they should be pleased with feeding on a boy. But I deem that those in this land, being themselves man-slayers, charge the Goddess with their own baseness, for I think not that any one of the Gods is bad.

CHORUS
Ye dark blue, dark blue meetings of the sea, which Io, hurried along by the brize, once passed through to the Euxine wave, having changed the territory of Asia for Europe,—who were they who left fair-watered Eurotas, flourishing in reeds, or the sacred founts of Dirce, and came, and came to the inhospitable land, where the daughter of Jove bedews her altars and column-girt temples with human blood? Of a truth by the surge-dashing oars of fir, worked on both sides, they sailed in a nautical carriage o'er the ocean waves, striving in the emulation after loved wealth in their houses. For darling hope is in dangers insatiate among men, who bear off the weight of riches, wandering in vain speculation on the wave and o'er barbarian cities. But to some there is a mind immoderate after riches, to others they come unsought. How did they pass through the rocks that run together, the ne'er resting beaches of Phineus, and the marine shore, running o'er the surge of Amphitrite,—where the choruses of the fifty daughters of Nereus entwine in the dance,—although with breezes that fill the sails, the creaking rudders resting at the poop, with southern gales or the breezes of Zephyr, to the bird-haunted land, the white beach, the glorious race-course of Achilles, near the Euxine Sea. Would that, according to my mistress' prayers, Helen, the dear daughter of Leda, might

sometime chance to come, quitting the city of Troy, that, having been drenched about the head with the blood-stained lustral dews, she might die by my mistress' hand, paying in turn an equal penalty for her death. Most joyfully then would we receive this news, if any one came sailing from the Grecian land, to make the toils of my hapless slavery to cease. And would that in my dreams I might tread in mine home and ancestral city, enjoying the hymns of delight, a joy shared with the prosperous. But hither they come, bound as to their two hands with chains, a new sacrifice for the Goddess. Be silent, my friends, for these first-fruits of the Greeks approach the temples, nor has the herdsman told a false tale. O reverend Goddess, if the city performs these things agreeably to thee, receive the sacrifice which, not hallowed among the Greeks, the custom of this place presents as a public offering.

IPHIGENIA

Be it so. I must first take care that the rites of the Goddess are as they should be. Let go the hands of the strangers, that being consecrated they may no longer be in bonds. And, going within the temple, make ready the things which are necessary and usual on these occasions. Alas! Who is the mother who once bore you? And who your father, and your sister, if there be any born? Of what a pair of youths deprived will she be brotherless! For all the dispensations of the Gods creep into obscurity, and no one absent knows misfortune, for fortune leads astray to what is hardly known. Whence come ye, O unhappy strangers? After how long a time have ye sailed to this land, and ye will be a long time from your home, ever among the shades!

ORESTES

Why mournest thou thus, and teasest us concerning our future ills, whoever thou art, O lady? In naught do I deem him wise, who, when about to die, with bewailings seeks to overcome the fear of death, nor him who deplores death now near at hand, when he has no hope of safety, in that he joins two ills instead of one, both incurs the charge of folly, and dies none the less. But one must needs let fortune take its course. But mourn us not, for we know and are acquainted with the sacrificial rites of this place.

IPHIGENIA

Which of ye twain here is named Pylades? This I would fain know first.

ORESTES

This man, if indeed 'tis any pleasure for thee to know this.

IPHIGENIA

Born citizen of what Grecian state?

ORESTES

And what wouldst thou gain by knowing this, lady?

IPHIGENIA

Are ye brothers from one mother?

ORESTES

In friendship we are, but we are not related, lady.

IPHIGENIA

But what name did the father who begot thee give to thee?

ORESTES

In truth we might be styled the unhappy.

IPHIGENIA
I ask not this. Leave this to fortune.

ORESTES
Dying nameless, I should not be mocked.

IPHIGENIA
Wherefore dost grudge this, and art thus proud?

ORESTES
My body thou shalt sacrifice, not my name.

IPHIGENIA
Nor wilt thou tell me which is thy city?

ORESTES
No. For thou seekest a thing of no profit, seeing I am to die.

IPHIGENIA
But what hinders thee from granting me this favor?

ORESTES
I boast renowned Argos for my country.

IPHIGENIA
In truth, by the Gods I ask thee, stranger, art thou thence born?

ORESTES
From Mycenæ, that was once prosperous.

IPHIGENIA
And hast thou set out a wanderer from thy country, or by what hap?

ORESTES
I flee in a certain wise unwilling, willingly.

IPHIGENIA
Wouldst thou tell me one thing that I wish?

ORESTES
That something, forsooth, may be added to my misfortune.

IPHIGENIA
And truly thou hast come desired by me, in coming from Argos.

ORESTES
Not by myself, at all events; but if by thee, do thou enjoy it.

IPHIGENIA

Perchance thou knowest Troy, the fame of which is every where.

ORESTES
Ay, would that I never had, not even seeing it in a dream!

IPHIGENIA
They say that it is now no more, and has fallen by the spear.

ORESTES
And so it is, nor have you heard what is not the case.

IPHIGENIA
And is Helen come back to the house of Menelaus?

ORESTES
She is, ay, coming unluckily to one of mine.

IPHIGENIA
And where is she? For she has incurred an old debt of evil with me also.

ORESTES
She dwells in Sparta with her former consort.

IPHIGENIA
O hateful pest among the Greeks, not to me only!

ORESTES
I also have received some fruits of her nuptials.

IPHIGENIA
And did the return of the Greeks take place, as is reported?

ORESTES
How dost thou question me, embracing all matters at once!

IPHIGENIA
For I wish to obtain this before that thou diest.

ORESTES
Examine me, since thou hast this longing, and I will speak.

IPHIGENIA
Has a certain seer named Calchas returned from Troy?

ORESTES
He perished, as the story ran, at Mycenæ.

IPHIGENIA
O revered Goddess, how well it is! And how fares the son of Laertes?

ORESTES

He has not yet returned to his home, but he is alive, as report goes.

IPHIGENIA
May he perish, never obtaining a return to his country!

ORESTES
Invoke nothing—all his affairs are in a sickly state.

IPHIGENIA
But is the son of Thetis, the daughter of Nereus, yet alive?

ORESTES
He is not. In vain he held his wedding in Aulis.

IPHIGENIA
A crafty wedding it was, as those who have suffered say.

ORESTES
Who canst thou be? How well dost ken the affairs of Greece!

IPHIGENIA
I am from thence. While yet a child I was undone.

ORESTES
With reason thou desirest to know the affairs there, O lady.

IPHIGENIA
But how fares the general, who they say is prosperous.

ORESTES
Who? For he whom I know is not of the fortunate.

IPHIGENIA
A certain king Agamemnon was called the son of Atreus.

ORESTES
I know not—cease from these words, O lady.

IPHIGENIA
Nay, by the Gods, but speak, that I may be rejoiced, O stranger.

ORESTES
The wretched one is dead, and furthermore hath ruined one.

IPHIGENIA
Is dead? By what mishap? O wretched me!

ORESTES
But why dost mourn this? Was he a relation of thine?

IPHIGENIA

I bemoan his former prosperity.

ORESTES
Ay, well mayest thou, for he has fallen, slain shamefully by a woman.

IPHIGENIA
O all grievous she that slew and he that fell!

ORESTES
Cease now at least, nor question further.

IPHIGENIA
Thus much at least, does the wife of the unhappy man live?

ORESTES
She is no more. The son she brought forth, he slew her.

IPHIGENIA
O house all troubled! with what intent, then?

ORESTES
Taking satisfaction on her for the death of his father.

IPHIGENIA
Alas! how well he executed an evil act of justice.

ORESTES
But, though just, he hath not good fortune from the Gods.

IPHIGENIA
But does Agamemnon leave any other child in his house?

ORESTES
He has left a single virgin daughter, Electra.

IPHIGENIA
What! Is there no report of his sacrificed daughter?

ORESTES
None indeed, save that being dead she beholds not the light.

IPHIGENIA
Hapless she, and the father who slew her!

ORESTES
She perished, a thankless offering because of a bad woman.

IPHIGENIA
But is the son of the deceased father at Argos?

ORESTES

He, wretched man, is nowhere and every where.

IPHIGENIA
Away, vain dreams, ye were then of naught!

ORESTES
Nor are the Gods who are called wise any less false than winged dreams. There is much inconsistency both among the Gods and among mortals. But one thing alone is left, when a man not being foolish, persuaded by the words of seers, has perished, as he hath perished in man's knowledge.

CHORUS
Alas! alas! But what of us and our fathers? Are they, or are they not in being, who can tell?

IPHIGENIA
Hear me, for I am come to a certain discourse, meditating what is at once profitable for you and me. But that which is well is chiefly produced thus, when the same matter pleases all. Would ye be willing, if I were to save you, to go to Argos, and bear a message for me to my friends there, and carry a letter, which a certain captive wrote, pitying me, nor deeming my hand that of a murderess, but that he died through custom, as the Goddess sanctioned such things as just? For I had no one who would go and bear the news back to Argos, and who, being preserved, would send my letters to some one of my friends. But do thou, for thou art, as thou seemest, of no ignoble birth, and knowest Mycenæ and the persons I wish, do thou, I say, be saved, receiving no dishonorable reward, your safety for the sake of trifling letters. But let this man, since the city compels it, be a sacrifice to the Goddess, apart from thee.

ORESTES
Well hast thou spoken the rest, save one thing, O stranger lady, for 'tis a heavy weight upon me that this man should be slain. For I was steersman of the vessel to these ills, but he is a fellow-sailor because of mine own troubles. In no wise then is it right that I should do thee a favor to his destruction, and myself escape from ills. But let it be thus. Give him the letter, for he will send it to Argos, so as to be well for thee, but let him that will slay me. Base is the man, who, casting his friends into calamity, himself is saved. But this man is a friend, who I fain should see the light no less that myself.

IPHIGENIA
O noblest spirit, how art thou sprung from some generous root, thou truly a friend to thy friends! Such might he be who is left of my brothers! For in good truth, strangers, I am not brotherless, save that I behold him not. But since thou willest thus, let us send this man bearing the letter, but thou wilt die, and some great desire of this chances to possess thee?

ORESTES
But who will sacrifice me, and dare this dreadful deed?

IPHIGENIA
I; for I have this sacrificial duty from the Goddess.

ORESTES
Unenviable indeed. O damsel, and unblest.

IPHIGENIA

But we lie under necessity, which one must beware.

ORESTES
Thyself, a female, sacrificing males with the sword?

IPHIGENIA
Not so; but I shall lave around thy head with the lustral stream.

ORESTES
But who is the slayer, if I may ask this?

IPHIGENIA
Within the house are they whose office is this.

ORESTES
And what manner of tomb will receive me, when I die?

IPHIGENIA
The holy flame within, and the dark chasm of the rock.

ORESTES
Alas! Would that a sister's hand might lay me out.

IPHIGENIA
A vain prayer hast thou uttered, whoever thou art, O stranger, for she dwells far from this barbarian land. Nevertheless, since thou art an Argive, I will not fail to do thee kindness in what is possible. For on thy tomb will I place much adornment, and with the tawny oil will I cause thy body to be soon consumed, and on thy pyre will I pour the flower-sucked riches of the swarthy bee. But I will go and fetch the letter from the shrines of the Goddess. But do thou not bear ill will against me. Guard them, ye servants, but without fetters. Perchance I shall send unexpected tidings to some one of my friends at Argos, whom I chiefly love, and the letter, telling to him that she lives whom he thinks dead, will announce a faithful pleasure.

CHORUS
I deplore thee now destined to the gory streams of the lustral waters.

ORESTES
'Tis piteous, truly; but fare ye well, stranger ladies.

CHORUS
But thee, [To **PYLADES**] O youth, we honor for thy happy fortune, that at some time thou wilt return to thy country.

PYLADES
Not to be coveted by friends, when friends are to die.

CHORUS
O mournful journeying! Alas! alas! thou art undone. Woe! woe! Which is the victim to be? For still my mind resolves twain doubtful ills, whether with groans I shall bemoan thee [To **ORESTES**] or thee [To **PYLADES**) first.

ORESTES

Pylades, hast thou, by the Gods, experienced the same feeling as myself?

PYLADES

I know not. Thou askest me unable to say.

ORESTES

Who is this damsel? With what a Grecian spirit she asked us concerning the toils in Troy, and the return of the Greeks, and Calchas wise in augury, and about Achilles, and how she pitied wretched Agamemnon, and asked me of his wife and children. This stranger lady is some Greek by race; for otherwise she never would have been sending a letter and making these inquiries, as sharing a common weal in the well-doing of Argos.

PYLADES

Thou hast outstripped me a little, but thou outstrippest me in saying the same things, save in one respect—for all, with whom there is any communication, know the fate of the king. But I was considering another subject.

ORESTES

What? laying it down in common, you will better understand.

PYLADES

'Tis base that I should behold the light, while you perish; and, having sailed with you, with you I must needs die also. For I shall incur the imputation of both cowardice and baseness in Argos and the Phocian land with its many dells, and I shall seem to the many, for the many are evil, to have arrived alone in safety to mine home, having deserted thee, or even to have murdered thee, taking advantage of the sickly state of thine house, and to have devised thy fate for the sake of reigning, in order that, forsooth, I might wed thy sister as an heiress. These things, then, I dread, and hold in shame, and it shall not be but I will breathe my last with thee, be slain, and have my body burned with thee, being a friend, and dreading reproach.

ORESTES

Speak words of better omen. I must needs bear my troubles, but when I may endure one single trouble, I will not endure twain. For what thou callest bitter and reproachful, that is my portion, if I cause thee to be slain who hast shared my toils. For, as far as I am concerned, it stands not badly with me, faring as I fare at the hands of the Gods, to end my life. But thou art prosperous, and hast a home pure, not sickening, but I have one impious and unhappy. And living thou mayest raise children from my sister, whom I gave thee to have as a wife, and my name might exist, nor would my ancestral house be ever blotted out. But go, live, and dwell in my father's house; and when thou comest to Greece and chivalrous Argos, by thy right hand, I commit to thee this charge. Heap up a tomb, and place upon it remembrances of me, and let my sister offer tears and her shorn locks upon my sepulchre. And tell how I died by an Argive woman's hand, sacrificed as an offering by the altar's side. And do thou never desert my sister, seeing my father's connections and home bereaved. And fare thee well! for I have found thee best among my friends. Oh thou who hast been my fellow-huntsman, my mate! Oh thou who hast borne the weight of many of my sorrows! But Phœbus, prophet though he be, has deceived me. For, artfully devising, he has driven me as far as possible from Greece, in shame of his former prophecies. To whom I, yielding up mine all, and obeying his words, having slain my mother, myself perish in turn.

PYLADES

Thou shalt have a tomb, and never will I, hapless one, betray thy sister's bed, since I shall hold thee more a friend dead than living. But the oracle of the God has never yet wronged thee, although thou art indeed on the very verge of death. But excessive mischance is very wont, is very wont to present changes, when the matter so falls.

ORESTES
Be silent—the words of Phœbus avail me naught, for the lady is coming hither without the temple.

IPHIGENIA
Depart ye, and go and make ready the things within for those who superintend the sacrifice. These, O stranger, are the many-folded inclosures of the letter, but hear thou what I further wish. No man is the same in trouble, and when he changes from fear into confidence. But I fear, lest he having got away from this land, will deem my letter of no account, who is about to bear this letter to Argos.

ORESTES
What wouldst thou? Concerning what art thou disturbed?

IPHIGENIA
Let him make me oath that he will ferry these writings to Argos, to those friends to whom I wish to send them.

ORESTES
Wilt thou in turn make the same assertion to him?

IPHIGENIA
That I will do, or will not do what thing? say.

ORESTES
That you will release him from this barbarian land, not dying.

IPHIGENIA
Thou sayest justly; for how could he bear the message?

ORESTES
But will the ruler also grant this?

IPHIGENIA
Yea. I will persuade him, and will myself embark him on the ship's hull.

ORESTES
Swear, but do thou commence such oath as is holy.

IPHIGENIA
Thou must say "I will give this letter to my friends."

PYLADES
I will give this letter to thy friends.

IPHIGENIA
And I will send thee safe beyond the Cyanean rocks.

PYLADES
Whom of the Gods dost thou call to witness of thine oath in these words?

IPHIGENIA
Diana, in whose temple I hold office.

PYLADES
But I call upon the king of heaven, hallowed Jove.

IPHIGENIA
But if, deserting thine oath, thou shouldst wrong me—

PYLADES
May I not return? But thou, if thou savest me not—

IPHIGENIA
May I never living set footprint in Argos.

PYLADES
Hear now then a matter which we have passed by.

IPHIGENIA
There will be opportunity hereafter, if matters stand aright.

PYLADES
Grant me this one exception. If the vessel suffer any harm, and the letter be lost in the storm, together with the goods, and I save my person only, that this mine oath be no longer valid.

IPHIGENIA
Knowest thou what I will do? for the many things contained in the folds of the letter bear opportunity for many things. I will tell you in words all that you are to convey to my friends, for this plan is safe. If indeed thou preservest the letter, it will itself silently tell the things written, but if these letters be lost at sea, saving thy body, thou wilt preserve my message.

PYLADES
Thou hast spoken well on behalf of the Gods and of myself. But tell me to whom at Argos I must needs bear these epistles, and what hearing from thee, I must tell.

IPHIGENIA
Bear word to Orestes, the son of Agamemnon, [Reading] "she that was sacrificed at Aulis gives this commission, Iphigenia alive, but no longer alive as far as those in Argos are concerned."

ORESTES
But where is she? Does she come back again having died?

IPHIGENIA
She, whom you see. Do not confuse me with speaking. [Continues reading] "Bear me to Argos, my brother, before I die, remove me from this barbarian land and the sacrifices of the Goddess, in which I have the office of slaying strangers."

ORESTES

Pylades, what shall I say? where shall we be found to be?

IPHIGENIA [Still reading]
"Or I will be a cause of curses upon thine house, Orestes," [With great stress upon the name and turning to **PYLADES**] "that thou, twice hearing the name, mayest know it."

PYLADES
O Gods!

IPHIGENIA
Why callest thou upon the Gods in matters that are mine?

PYLADES
'Tis nothing. Go on. I was wandering to another subject. Perchance, inquiring of thee, I shall arrive at things incredible.

IPHIGENIA [Continues reading]
"Say that the Goddess Diana saved me, giving in exchange for me a hind, which my father sacrificed, thinking that it was upon me that he laid the sharp sword, and she placed me to dwell in this land." This is the burden of my message, these are the words written in my letter.

PYLADES
O thou who hast secured me in easy oaths, and hast sworn things fairest, I will not delay much time, but I will firmly accomplish the oath I have sworn. Behold, I bear and deliver to thee a letter, O Orestes, from this thy sister.

ORESTES
I receive it. And letting go the opening of the letter, I will first seize a delight not in words—

[Attempts to embrace her.

O dearest sister mine, in amazement, yet nevertheless embracing thee with a doubting arm, I go to a source of delight, hearing things marvelous to me.

CHORUS
Stranger, thou dost not rightly pollute the servant of the Goddess, casting thine arm around her garments that should ne'er be touched.

ORESTES
O fellow-sister born of one sire, Agamemnon, turn not from me, possessing a brother whom you never thought to possess.

IPHIGENIA
I possess thee my brother? Wilt not cease speaking? Both Argos and Nauplia are frequented by him.

ORESTES
Unhappy one! thy brother is not there.

IPHIGENIA
But did the Lacedæmonian daughter of Tyndarus beget thee?

ORESTES

Ay, to the grandson of Pelops, whence I am sprung.

IPHIGENIA

What sayest thou? Hast thou any proof of this for me?

ORESTES

I have. Ask something relative to my ancestral home.

IPHIGENIA

Thou must needs then speak, and I learn.

ORESTES

I will first speak from hearsay from Electra, this. Thou knowest the strife that took place between Atreus and Thyestes?

IPHIGENIA

I have heard of it, when it was waged concerning the golden lamb.

ORESTES

Dost thou then remember weaving a representation of this on the deftly-wrought web?

IPHIGENIA

O dearest one. Thou art turning thy course near to my own thoughts.

ORESTES

And dost thou remember a picture on the loom, the turning away of the sun?

IPHIGENIA

I wove this image also in the fine-threaded web.

ORESTES

And didst thou receive a bath from thy mother, sent to Aulis?

IPHIGENIA

I know it: for the wedding, though good, did not take away my recollection.

ORESTES

But what? Dost thou remember to have given thine hair to be carried to thy mother?

IPHIGENIA

Ay, as a memorial for the tomb in place of my body.

ORESTES

But the proofs which I have myself beheld, these will I tell, viz. the ancient spear of Pelops in my father's house, which brandishing in his hand, he, Pelops, won Hippodameia, having slain Ænomaus, which is hidden in thy virgin chamber.

IPHIGENIA

O dearest one, no more, for thou art dearest. I hold thee, Orestes, one darling son far away from his father-land, from Argos, O thou dear one!

ORESTES

And I hold thee that wast dead, as was supposed. But tears, yet tearless, and groans together mingled with joy, bedew thine eyelids, and mine in like manner.

IPHIGENIA

This one, this, yet a babe I left, young in the arms of the nurse, ay, young in our house. O thou more fortunate than my words can tell, what shall I say? This matter has turned out beyond marvel or calculation.

ORESTES

Say this. May we for the future be happy with each other!

IPHIGENIA

I have experienced an unaccountable delight, dear companions, but I fear lest it flit from my hands, and escape toward the sky. O ye Cyclopean hearths, O Mycenæ, dear country mine. I am grateful to thee for my life, and grateful for my nurture, in that thou hast trained for me this brother light in my home.

ORESTES

In our race we are fortunate, but as to calamities, O sister, our life is by nature unhappy.

IPHIGENIA

But I wretched remember when my father with foolish spirit laid the sword upon my neck.

ORESTES

Ah me! For I seem, not being present, to behold you there.

IPHIGENIA

Without Hymen, O my brother, when I was being led to the fictitious nuptial bed of Achilles. But near the altar were tears and lamentations. Alas! alas, for the lustral waters there!

ORESTES

I mourn aloud for the deed my father dared.

IPHIGENIA

I obtained a fatherless, a fatherless lot. But one calamity follows upon another.

ORESTES

Ay, if thou hadst lost thy brother, O hapless one, by the intervention of some demon.

IPHIGENIA

O miserable for my dreadful daring! I have dared horrid, I have dared horrid things. Alas! my brother. But by a little hast thou escaped an unholy destruction, stricken by my hands. But what will be the end after this? What fortune will befall me? What retreat can I find for thee away from this city? can I send you out of the reach of slaughter to your country Argos, before that my sword enter on the contest concerning thy blood? This is thy business, O hapless soul, to discover, whether over the land, not in a ship, but by the gust of your feet thou wilt approach death, passing through barbarian hordes, and through ways not to be traversed? Or wilt thou pass through the Cyanean creek, a long journey in the flight of ships. Wretched, wretched one! Who then or God, or mortal, or unexpected event, having accomplished a way out of inextricable difficulties, will show forth to the sole twain Atrides a release from ills?

CHORUS
Among marvels and things passing even fable are these things which I shall tell as having myself beheld, and not from hearsay.

PYLADES
It is meet indeed that friends coming into the presence of friends, Orestes, should embrace one another with their hands, but, having ceased from mournful matters, it behooves you also to betake you to those measures by which we, obtaining the glorious name of safety, may depart from this barbarian earth. For it is the part of wise men, not wandering from their present chance, when they have obtained an opportunity, to acquire further delights.

ORESTES
Thou sayest well. But I think that fortune will take care of this with us. For if a man be zealous, it is likely that the divine power will have still greater power.

IPHIGENIA
Do not restrain or hinder me from your words, not first to know what fortune of life Electra has obtained, for this were pleasant to me to hear.

ORESTES
She is partner with this man, possessing a happy life.

IPHIGENIA
And of what country is he, and son of what man born?

ORESTES
Strophius the Phocian is styled his father.

IPHIGENIA
And he is of the daughter of Atreus, a relative of mine?

ORESTES
Ay, a cousin, my only certain friend.

IPHIGENIA
Was he not in being, when my father sought to slay me?

ORESTES
He was not, for Strophius was childless some time.

IPHIGENIA
Hail! O thou spouse of my sister.

ORESTES
Ay, and my preserver, not relation only.

IPHIGENIA
But how didst thou dare the terrible deeds in respect to your mother?

ORESTES

Let us be silent respecting my mother—'twas in avenging my father.

IPHIGENIA

And what was the reason for her slaying her husband?

ORESTES

Let go the subject of my mother. Nor is it pleasant for you to hear.

IPHIGENIA

I am silent. But Argos now looks up to thee.

ORESTES

Menelaus rules: I am an exile from my country.

IPHIGENIA

What, did our uncle abuse our house unprospering?

ORESTES

Not so, but the fear of the Erinnyes drives me from my land.

IPHIGENIA

For this then wert thou spoken of as being frantic even here on the shore.

ORESTES

We were beheld not now for the first time in a hapless state.

IPHIGENIA

I perceive. The Goddesses goaded thee on because of thy mother.

ORESTES

Ay, so as to cast a bloody bit upon me.

IPHIGENIA

For wherefore didst thou pilot thy foot to this land?

ORESTES

I came, commanded by the oracles of Phœbus—

IPHIGENIA

To do what thing? Is it one to be spoken of or kept in silence?

ORESTES

I will tell you, but these are the beginning for me of many woes. After these evil things concerning my mother, on which I keep silence, had been wrought, I was driven an exile by the pursuits of the Erinnyes, when Loxias sent my foot to Athens, that I might render satisfaction to the deities that must not be named. For there is a holy council, that Jove once on a time instituted for Mars on account of some pollution of his hands. And coming thither, at first indeed no one of the strangers received me willingly, as being abhorred by the Gods, but they who had respect to me, afforded me a stranger's meal at a separate table, being under the same house roof, and silently devised in respect to me, unaddressed by them, how I might be separated from their banquet and cup, and, having filled up a share of wine in a separate vessel, equal for all, they enjoyed themselves. And I did not think fit to rebuke my guests, but I grieved in silence, and did not seem to perceive their conduct, deeply groaning, because I was my mother's slayer. But I hear that my misfortunes have been made a festival at Athens, and that this custom still remains, that the people of Pallas honor the Libation Vessel. But when I came to the hill of Mars, and stood in judgment, I indeed occupying one seat, but the eldest of the Erinnyes the other, having spoken and heard respecting my mother's death, Phœbus saved me by bearing witness, but Pallas counted out for me the equal votes with her hand, and I came off victor in the bloody trial. As many then as sat in judgment, persuaded by the sentence, determined to hold their dwelling near the court itself. But as many of the Erinnyes as did not yield obedience to the sentence passed, continually kept driving me with unsettled wanderings, until I again returned to the holy ground of Phœbus, and lying stretched before the adyts, hungering for food, I swore that I would break from life by dying on the spot, unless Phœbus, who had undone, should preserve me. Upon this Phœbus, uttering a voice from the golden tripod, sent me hither to seize the heaven-sent image, and place it in the land of Athens. But that safety which he marked out for me do thou aid in. For if we can lay hold on the image of the Goddess, I both shall cease from my madness, and embarking thee in the bark of many oars, I shall settle thee again in Mycenæ. But, O beloved one, O sister mine, preserve my ancestral home, and preserve me, since all my state and that of the Pelopids is undone, unless we seize on the heavenly image of the Goddess.

CHORUS
Some dreadful wrath of the Gods hath burst forth, and leads the seed of Tantalus through troubles.

IPHIGENIA
I entertained the desire to reach Argos, and behold thee, my brother, even before thou camest. But I wish, as you do, both to save thee, and to restore again our sickening ancestral home from troubles, in no wise wrath with him who would have slain me. For I should both release my hand from thy slaughter, and preserve mine house. But I fear how I shall be able to escape the notice of the Goddess and the king, when he shall find the stone pedestal bared of the image. And how shall I escape death? What account can I give? But if indeed these matters can be effected at once, and thou wilt bear away the image, and lead me in the fair-pooped ship, the risk will be a glorious one. But separated from this I perish, but you, arranging your own affairs, would obtain a prosperous return. Yet in no wise will I fly, not even if I needs must perish, having preserved thee. In no wise, I say; for a man who dies from among his household is regretted, but a woman is of little account.

ORESTES
I would not be the murderer both of thee and of my mother. Her blood is enough, and being of the same mind with you, with you I should wish, living or dying, to obtain an equal lot. But I will lead thee, even though I myself fall here, to my house, or, remaining with thee, will die. But hear my opinion. If this had been disagreeable to Diana, how would Loxias have answered, that I should remove the image of the Goddess to the city of Pallas, and behold thy face? For, putting all these matters together, I hope to obtain a return.

IPHIGENIA
How then can it happen that neither you die, and that we obtain what we wish? For it is in this respect that our journey homeward is at fault, but the will is not wanting.

ORESTES
Could we possibly destroy the tyrant?

IPHIGENIA

Thou tellest a fearful thing, for strangers to slay their receivers.

ORESTES
But if it will preserve thee and me, one must run the risk.

IPHIGENIA
I could not—yet I approve your zeal.

ORESTES
But what if you were secretly to hide me in this temple?

IPHIGENIA
In order, forsooth, that, taking advantage of darkness, we might be saved?

ORESTES
For night is the time for thieves, the light for truth.

IPHIGENIA
But within are the sacred keepers, whom we can not escape.

ORESTES
Alas! we are undone. How can we then be saved?

IPHIGENIA
I seem to have a certain new device.

ORESTES
Of what kind? Make me a sharer in your opinion, that I also may learn.

IPHIGENIA
I will make use of thy ravings as a contrivance.

ORESTES
Ay, cunning are women to find out tricks.

IPHIGENIA
I will say that thou, being slayer of thy mother, art come from Argos.

ORESTES
Make use of my troubles, if you can turn them to account.

IPHIGENIA
I will say that it is not lawful to sacrifice thee to the Goddess.

ORESTES
Having what pretext? For I partly suspect.

IPHIGENIA
As not being pure, but I will say that I will give what is holy to sacrifice.

ORESTES

How then the more will the image of the Goddess be obtained?

IPHIGENIA
I will say that I will purify thee in the fountains of the sea.

ORESTES
The statue, in quest of which, we have sailed, is still in the temple.

IPHIGENIA
And I will say that I must wash that too, as if you had laid hands on it.

ORESTES
Where then is the damp breaker of the sea of which you speak?

IPHIGENIA
Where thy ship rides at anchor with rope-bound chains.

ORESTES
But wilt thou, or some one else, bear the image in their hands?

IPHIGENIA
I, for it is lawful for me alone to touch it.

ORESTES
But in what part of this contrivance will our friend Pylades be placed?

IPHIGENIA
He will be said to bear the same pollution of hands as thyself.

ORESTES
And wilt thou do this unknown to, or with the knowledge of the king?

IPHIGENIA
Having persuaded him by words, for I could not escape notice.

ORESTES
And truly the well-rowed ship is ready for sailing.

IPHIGENIA
You must take care of the rest, that it be well.

ORESTES
There lacks but one thing, namely, that these women who are present preserve our secret. But do thou beseech them, and find words that will persuade. A woman in truth has power to move pity. But all the rest will perchance fall out well.

IPHIGENIA
O dearest women, I look to you, and my affairs rest in you, as to whether they turn out well, or be of naught, and I be deprived of my country, my dear brother, and dearest sister. And let this first be the commencement of my words. We are women, a race well inclined to one another, and most safe in keeping secret matters of common interest. Do ye keep silence for us, and labor out our escape.

Honorable is it for the man who possesses a faithful tongue. But behold how one fortune holds the three most dear, either a return to our father-land, or to die. But, being preserved, that thou also mayest share my fortune, I will restore thee safe to Greece. But, by thy right hand, thee, and thee [Addressing the **WOMEN of the CHORUS** in succession] I beseech, and thee by thy beloved cheek, and thy knees, and those most dear at home, mother, and father, and children, to whom there are such. What say ye? Who of you will, or will not speak! these things. For if ye assent not to my words, I am undone, and my wretched sister.

CHORUS
Be of good cheer, dear mistress, and think only of being saved, since on my part all shall be kept secret, the mighty Jove be witness! in the things thou enjoinest.

IPHIGENIA
May your words profit ye, and may ye be blest. 'Tis thy part now, and thine [To the different **WOMEN**] to enter the house, as the ruler of this land will straightway come, inquiring concerning the sacrifice of the strangers, whether it is over. O revered Goddess, who in the recesses of Aulis didst save me from the dire hand of a slaying father, now also save me and these, or the voice of Loxias will through thee be no longer truthful among mortals. But do thou with good will quit the barbarian land for Athens, for it becomes thee not to dwell here, when you can possess a blest city.

CHORUS
Thou bird, that by the rocky cliffs of the sea, halcyon, dost chant thy mournful elegy, a sound well understood by the skilled, namely, that thou art ever bemoaning thine husband in song, I, a wingless bird, compare my dirge with thine, longing for the assemblies of the Greeks, longing for Lucina, who dwells along the Cynthian height, and near the palm with its luxuriant foliage, and the rich-springing laurel, and the holy shoot of the deep blue olive, the dear place of Latona's throes, and the lake that rolls its waters in a circle, where the melodious swan honors the muses. O ye many tricklings of tears which fell upon my cheeks, when, our towers being destroyed, I traveled in ships beneath the oars and the spears of the foes. And through a bartering of great price I came a journey to a barbarian land, where I serve the daughter of Agamemnon, the priestess of the Goddess, and the sheep-slaughtering altars, envying her who has all her life been unfortunate; for she bends not under necessity, who is familiar with it. Unhappiness is wont to change, but to fare ill after prosperity is a heavy life for mortals. And thee indeed, O mistress, an Argive ship of fifty oars will conduct home, and the wax-bound reed of mountain Pan with Syrinx tune cheer on the oarsmen, and prophet Phœbus, plying the tones of his seven-stringed lyre, with song will lead thee prosperously to the rich land of Athens. But leaving me here thou wilt travel by the dashing oars. And the halyards by the prow, will stretch forth the sails to the air, above the beak, the sheet lines of the swift-journeying ship. Would that I might pass through the glittering course, where the fair light of the sun wends its way, and over my own chamber might rest from rapidly moving the pinions on my shoulders. And would that I might stand in the dance, where also I was wont to stand, a virgin sprung from honorable nuptials, wreathing the dances of my companions at the foot of my dear mother, bounding to the rivalry of the graces, to the wealthy strife respecting beauteous hair, pouring my variously-painted garb and tresses around, I shadowed my cheeks.

[Enter **THOAS**.

THOAS
Where is the Grecian woman who keeps the gate of this temple? Has she yet begun the sacrifice of the strangers, and are the bodies burning in the flame within the pure recesses?

CHORUS

Here she is, O king, who will tell thee clearly all.

THOAS
Ah! Why art thou removing in your arms this image of the Goddess from its seat that may not be disturbed, O daughter of Agamemnon?

IPHIGENIA
O king, rest there thy foot in the portico.

THOAS
But what new matter is in the house, Iphigenia?

IPHIGENIA
I avert the ill—for holy do I utter this word.

THOAS
What new thing art thou prefacing? speak clearly.

IPHIGENIA
O king, no pure offerings hast thou hunted out for me.

THOAS
What hath taught you this? or dost thou speak it as matter of opinion?

IPHIGENIA
The image of the Goddess hath again turned away from her seat.

THOAS
Of its own accord, or did an earthquake turn it?

IPHIGENIA
Of its own accord, and it closed its eyes.

THOAS
But what is the cause? is it pollution from the strangers?

IPHIGENIA
That very thing, naught else, for they have done dreadful things.

THOAS
What, did they slay any of the barbarians upon the shore?

IPHIGENIA
They came possessing the stain of domestic murder.

THOAS
What? for I am fallen into a longing to learn this.

IPHIGENIA
They put an end to a mother's life by conspiring sword.

THOAS
Apollo! not even among barbarians would any one have dared this.

IPHIGENIA
By persecutions they were driven out of all Greece.

THOAS
Is it then on their account that thou bearest the image without?

IPHIGENIA
Ay, under the holy sky, that I may remove it from blood stains.

THOAS
But how didst thou discover the pollution of the strangers?

IPHIGENIA
I examined them, when the image of the Goddess turned away.

THOAS
Greece hath trained thee up wise, in that thou well didst perceive this.

IPHIGENIA
And now they have cast out a delightful bait for my mind.

THOAS
By telling thee any charming news of those at Argos?

IPHIGENIA
That my only brother Orestes fares well.

THOAS
So that, forsooth, thou mightest preserve them because of their pleasant news!

IPHIGENIA
And that my father lives and fares well.

THOAS
But thou hast with reason attended to the interest of the Goddess.

IPHIGENIA
Ay, because hating all Greece that destroyed me.

THOAS
What then shall we do, say, concerning the two strangers?

IPHIGENIA
We needs must respect the established law.

THOAS
Are not the lustral waters and thy sword already engaged?

IPHIGENIA

First I would fain lave them in pure cleansings.

THOAS

In the fountains of waters, or in the dew of the sea?

IPHIGENIA

The sea washes out all the ills of men.

THOAS

They would certainly fall in a more holy manner before the Goddess.

IPHIGENIA

And my matters would be in a more fitting state.

THOAS

Does not the wave dash against the very temple?

IPHIGENIA

There is need of solitude, for we have other things to do.

THOAS

Lead them whither thou wilt, I crave not to see things that may not be told.

IPHIGENIA

The image of the Goddess also must be purified by me.

THOAS

If indeed the stain of the matricide hath fallen on it.

IPHIGENIA

For otherwise I should not have removed it from its pedestal.

THOAS

Just piety and foresight! How reasonably doth all the city marvel at thee!

IPHIGENIA

Knowest thou then what must be done for me?

THOAS

'Tis thine to explain this.

IPHIGENIA

Cast fetters upon the strangers.

THOAS

Whither could they escape from thee?

IPHIGENIA

Greece knows nothing faithful.

THOAS
Go for the fetters, attendants.

IPHIGENIA
Ay, and let them bring the strangers hither.

THOAS
This shall be.

IPHIGENIA
Having enveloped their heads in robes.

THOAS
Against the scorching of the sun?

IPHIGENIA
And send thou with me of thy followers—

THOAS
These shall accompany thee.

IPHIGENIA
And send some one to signify to the city—

THOAS
What hap?

IPHIGENIA
That all remain in their homes.

THOAS
Lest they encounter homicide?

IPHIGENIA
For such things are unclean.

THOAS
Go thou, and order this.

IPHIGENIA
That no one come into sight.

THOAS
Thou carest well for the city.

IPHIGENIA
Ay, and more particularly friends must not be present.

THOAS
This you say in reference to me.

IPHIGENIA
But do thou, abiding here before the temple of the Goddess—

THOAS
Do what?

IPHIGENIA
Purify the house with a torch.

THOAS
That it may be pure when thou comest back to it?

IPHIGENIA
But when the strangers come out,

THOAS
What must I do?

IPHIGENIA
Place your garment before your eyes.

THOAS
Lest I contract contagion?

IPHIGENIA
But if I seem to tarry very long,

THOAS
What limit of this shall I have?

IPHIGENIA
Wonder at nothing.

THOAS
Do thou rightly the business of the Goddess at thy leisure.

IPHIGENIA
And may this purification turn out as I wish!

THOAS
I join in your prayer.

IPHIGENIA
I now see these strangers coming out of the house, and the adornments of the Goddess, and the young lambs, in order that I may wash out foul slaughter by slaughter, and the shining light of lamps, and the other things, as many as I ordered as purifications for the strangers and the Goddess. But I proclaim to the strangers to get out of the way of this pollution, if any gate-keeper of the temples keeps pure hands for the Gods, or is about to join in nuptial alliance, or is pregnant, flee, get out of the way, lest this pollution fall on any. O thou queen, virgin daughter of Jove and Latona, if I wash away the blood-pollution from these men, and sacrifice where 'tis fitting, thou wilt occupy a pure

house, and we shall be prosperous. But although I do not speak of the rest, I nevertheless signify my meaning to the Gods who know most things, and to thee, O Goddess.

CHORUS
Of noble birth is the offspring of Latona, whom once on a time in the fruitful valleys of Delos, Phœbus with his golden locks, skilled on the lyre, (and she who rejoices in skill of the bow,) his mother bore while yet an infant from the sea-side rock, leaving the renowned place of her delivery, destitute of waters, the Parnassian height haunted by Bacchus, where the ruddy-visaged serpent, with spotted back, brazen beneath the shady laurel with its rich foliage, an enormous prodigy of the earth, guarded the subterranean oracle. Him thou, O Phœbus, while yet an infant, while yet leaping in thy dear mother's arms, didst slay, and entered upon thy divine oracles, and thou sittest on the golden tripod, on the throne that is ever true, distributing to mortals prophecies from the divine adyts beneath the Castalian streams, dwelling hard by, occupying a dwelling in the middle of the earth. But when, having gone against Themis, daughter of earth, he expelled her from the divine oracles, earth begot dark phantoms of dreams, which to many mortals explain what first, what afterward, what in future will happen, during their sleep in the couches of the dusky earth. But the earth deprived Phœbus of the honor of prophecies, through anger on her daughter's account, and the swift-footed king, hastening to Olympus, stretched forth his little hand to the throne of Jove. Beseeching him to take away the earth-born wrath of the Goddess, and the nightly responses. But he laughed, because his son had come quickly to him, wishing to obtain the wealthy office, and he shook his hair, and put an end to the nightly dreams, and took away nightly divination from mortals, and again conferred the honor on Loxias, and confidence to mortals from the songs of oracles proclaimed on this throne, thronged to by many strangers.

[Enter a **MESSENGER**.

MESSENGER
O ye guardians of the temple and presidents of the altars, where in this land has king Thoas gone? Do ye, opening the well-fastened gates, call the ruler of this land outside the house.

CHORUS
But what is it, if I may speak when I am not bidden?

MESSENGER
The two youths have escaped, and are gone by the contrivances of Agamemnon's daughter, endeavoring to fly from this land, and taking the sacred image in the bosom of a Grecian ship.

CHORUS
Thou tellest an incredible story, but the king of this country, whom you wish to see, is gone, having quitted the temple.

MESSENGER
Whither? For he needs must know what has been done.

CHORUS
We know not. But go thou and pursue him to wheresoever, having met with him, thou mayest recount this news.

MESSENGER
See, how faithless is the female race! and ye are partners in what has been done.

CHORUS
Art thou mad? What have we to do with the flight of the strangers? Will you not go as quickly as possible to the gates of the rulers?

MESSENGER
Not at least before some distinct informer tell me this, whether the ruler of the land is within or not within. Ho there! Open the fastenings, I speak to those within, and tell the master that I am at the gates, bearing a weight of evil news.

THOAS [Coming out]
Who makes this noise near the temple of the Goddess, hammering at the door, and sending fear within?

MESSENGER
These women told me falsely, and tried to drive me from the house, that you were away, while you really were in the house.

THOAS
Expecting or hunting after what gain?

MESSENGER
I will afterward tell of what concerns them, but hear the present, immediate matter. The virgin, she that presided over the altars here, Iphigenia, has gone out of the land with the strangers, having the sacred image of the Goddess; but the expiations were pretended.

THOAS
How sayest thou? possessed by what breath of calamity?

MESSENGER
In order to preserve Orestes, for at this thou wilt marvel.

THOAS
What Orestes? Him, whom the daughter of Tyndarus bore?

MESSENGER
Him whom she consecrated to the Goddess at these altars.

THOAS
Oh marvel! How can I rightly call thee by a greater name?

MESSENGER
Do not turn thine attention to this, but listen to me; and having perceived and heard, clearly consider what pursuit will catch the strangers.

THOAS
Speak, for thou sayest well, for they do not flee by the way of the neighboring sea, so as to be able to escape my fleet.

MESSENGER
When we came to the sea-shore, where the vessel of Orestes was anchored in secret, to us indeed, whom thou didst send with her, bearing fetters for the strangers, the daughter of Agamemnon made

signs that we should get far out of the way, as she was about to offer the secret flame and expiation, for which she had come. But she, holding the fetters of the strangers in her hands, followed behind them. And these matters were suspicious, but they satisfied your attendants, O king. But at length, in order forsooth that she might seem to us to be doing something, she screamed aloud, and chanted barbarian songs like a sorceress, as if washing out the stain of murder. But after we had remained sitting a long time, it occurred to us whether the strangers set at liberty might not slay her, and take to flight. And through fear lest we might behold what was not fitting, we sat in silence, but at length the same words were in every body's mouth, that we should go to where they were, although not permitted. And upon this we behold the hull of the Grecian ship, the rowing winged with well-fitted oars, and fifty sailors holding their oars in the tholes, and the youths, freed from their fetters, standing on the shore astern of the ship. But some held in the prow with their oars, and others from the epotides let down the anchor, and others hastily applying the ladders, drew the stern-cables through their hands, and giving them to the sea, let them down to the strangers. But we unsparing of the toil, when we beheld the crafty stratagem, laid hold of the female stranger and of the cables, and tried to drag the rudders from the fair-prowed ship from the steerage-place. But words ensued: "On what plea do ye take to the sea, stealing from this land the images and priestess? Whose son art thou, who thyself, who art carrying this woman from the land?" But he replied, "Orestes, her brother, that you may know, the son of Agamemnon, I, having taken this my sister, whom I had lost from my house, am bearing her off." But naught the less we clung to the female stranger, and compelled them by force to follow us to thee, upon which arose sad smitings of the cheeks. For they had not arms in their hands, nor had we; but fists were sounding against fists, and the arms of both the youths at once were aimed against our sides and to the liver, so that we at once were exhausted and worn out in our limbs. But stamped with horrid marks we fled to a precipice, some having bloody wounds on the head, others in the eyes, and standing on the heights, we waged a safer warfare, and pelted stones. But archers, standing on the poop, hindered us with their darts, so that we returned back. And meanwhile—for a tremendous wave drove the ship against the land, and there was alarm on board lest she might dip her sheet-line—Orestes, taking his sister on his left shoulder, walked into the sea, and leaping upon the ladder, placed her within the well-banked ship, and also the image of the daughter of Jove, that fell from heaven. And from the middle of the ship a voice spake thus, "O mariners of the Grecian ship, seize on your oars, and make white the surge, for we have obtained the things on account of which we sailed o'er the Euxine within the Symplegades." But they shouting forth a pleasant cry, smote the brine. The ship, as long indeed as it was within the port, went on; but, passing the outlet, meeting with a strong tide, it was driven back. For a terrible gale coming suddenly, drives the bark winged with well-fitted oars poop-wise, but they persevered, kicking against the wave, but an ebbing tide brought them again aground. But the daughter of Agamemnon stood up and prayed, "O daughter of Latona, bring me, thy priestess, safe into Greece from a barbarian land, and pardon the stealing away of me. Thou also, O Goddess, lovest thy brother, and think thou that I also love my kindred." But the sailors shouted a pæan in assent to the prayers of the girl, applying on a given signal the point of the shoulders, bared from their hands, to the oars. But more and more the vessel kept nearing the rocks, and one indeed leaped into the sea with his feet, and another fastened woven nooses. And I was immediately sent hither to thee, to tell thee, O king, what had happened there. But go, taking fetters and halters in your hands, for, unless the wave shall become tranquil, there is no hope of safety for the strangers. For the ruler of the sea, the revered Neptune, both favorably regards Troy, and is at enmity with the Pelopidæ. And he will now, as it seems, deliver up to thee and the citizens the son of Agamemnon, to take him into your hands, and his sister, who is detected ungratefully forgetting the Goddess in respect to the sacrifice at Aulis.

CHORUS
O hapless Iphigenia, with thy brother wilt thou die, again coming into the hands of thy masters.

THOAS

O all ye citizens of this barbarian land, will ye not, casting bridles on your horses, run to the shore, and receive the casting on of the Grecian ship? But hastening, by the favor of the Goddess, will ye not hunt down the impious men, and some of you haul the swift barks down to the sea, that by sea, and by horse-coursings on the land seizing them, we may either hurl them down the broken rock, or impale their bodies upon stakes. But you women, the accomplices in these plots, I will punish hereafter, when I have leisure, but now, having such a present duty, we will not remain idle.

[**MINERVA** appears.

MINERVA

Whither, whither sendest thou this troop to follow the fugitives, king Thoas? List to the words of me, Minerva. Cease pursuing, and stirring on the onset of your host. For by the destined oracles of Loxias Orestes came hither, fleeing the wrath of the Erinnyes, and in order to conduct his sister's person to Argos, and to bear the sacred image into my land, by way of respite from his present troubles. Thus are our words for thee, but as to him, Orestes, whom you wish to slay, having caught him in a tempest at sea, Neptune has already, for my sake, rendered the surface of the sea waveless, piloting him along in the ship. But do thou, Orestes, learning my commands, (for thou hearest the voice of a Goddess, although not present,) go, taking the image and thy sister. And when thou art come to heaven-built Athens, there is a certain sacred district in the farthest bounds of Atthis, near the Carystian rock, which my people call Aloe—here, having built a temple, do thou enshrine the image named after the Tauric land and thy toils, which thou hast labored through, wandering over Greece, under the goad of the Erinnyes. But mortals hereafter shall celebrate her as the Tauric Goddess Diana. And do thou ordain this law, that, when the people celebrate a feast in grateful commemoration of thy release from slaughter, let them apply the sword to the neck of a man, and let blood flow on account of the holy Goddess, that she may have honor. But, O Iphigenia, thou must needs be guardian of the temple of this Goddess at the hallowed ascent of Brauron; where also thou shalt be buried at thy death, and they shall offer to you the honor of rich woven vestments, which women, dying in childbed, may leave in their houses. But I command thee to let these Grecian women depart from the land on account of their disinterested disposition, I, having saved thee also on a former occasion, by determining the equal votes in the Field of Mars, Orestes, and that, according to the same law, he should conquer, whoever receive equal suffrages. But, O son of Agamemnon, do thou remove thy sister from this land, nor be thou angered, Thoas.

THOAS

Queen Minerva, whosoever, on hearing the words of the Gods, is disobedient, thinks not wisely. But I will not be angry with Orestes, if he has carried away the image of the Goddess with him, nor with his sister. For what credit is there in contending with the potent Gods? Let them depart to thy land with the image of the Goddess, and let them prosperously enshrine the effigy. But I will also send these women to blest Greece, as thy mandate bids. And I will stop the spear which I raised against the strangers, and the oars of the ships, as this seems fit to thee, O Goddess.

MINERVA

I commend your words, for fate commands both thee and the Gods themselves. Go, ye breezes, conduct the vessel of Agamemnon's son to Athens. And I will journey with you, to guard the hallowed image of my sister.

CHORUS

Go ye, happy because of your preserved fortune. But, O Athenian Pallas, hallowed among both immortals and mortals, we will do even as thou biddest. For I have received a very delightful and unhoped-for voice in my hearing. O thou all hallowed Victory, mayest thou possess my life, and cease not to crown it.

Euripides is rightly lauded as one of the great dramatists of all time. In his lifetime, he wrote over 90 plays and although only 18 have survived they reveal the scope and reach of his genius.

Euripides is identified with many theatrical innovations that have influenced drama all the way down to modern times, especially in the representation of traditional, mythical heroes as ordinary people in extraordinary circumstances. This new approach led him to pioneer developments that later writers would adapt to comedy. Yet he also became "the most tragic of poets", focusing on the inner lives and motives of his characters in a way previously unknown. He was "the creator of...that cage which is the theatre of Shakespeare's Othello, Racine's Phèdre, of Ibsen and Strindberg," in which "...imprisoned men and women destroy each other by the intensity of their loves and hates", and yet he was also the literary ancestor of comic dramatists as diverse as Menander and George Bernard Shaw.

As would be expected from a life lived 2,500 years ago, details of it are few and far between. Accounts of his life, written down the ages, do exist but whether much is reliable or surmised is open to debate.

Most accounts agree that he was born on Salamis Island around 480 BC, to mother Cleito and father Mnesarchus, a retailer who lived in a village near Athens. Upon the receipt of an oracle saying that his son was fated to win "crowns of victory", Mnesarchus insisted that the boy should train for a career in athletics.

His education was not only confined to athletics: he also studied painting and philosophy under the masters Prodicus and Anaxagoras.

However, what became quickly very clear was that athletics was not to be his way to win crowns of victory. Euripides had been lucky enough to have been born in the era as the other two masters of Greek Tragedy; Sophocles and Æschylus. It was in their footsteps that he was destined to follow.

His first play was performed some thirteen years after the first of Socrates plays and a mere three years after Æschylus had written his classic The Oristria.

Theatre was becoming a very important part of the Greek culture. The Dionysia, held annually, was the most important festival of theatre and second only to the fore-runner of the Olympic games, the Panathenia, held every four years, in its appeal. It was a large festival in ancient Athens in honor of the god Dionysus, the central events of which were the theatrical performances of dramatic tragedies and, from 487 BC, comedies. The Dionysia actually consisted of two related festivals, the Rural Dionysia and the City Dionysia, which took place in different parts of the year.

Euripides first competed in the City Dionysia, in 455 BC, one year after the death of Æschylus, and, incredibly, it was not until 441 BC that he won first prize. His final competition in Athens was in 408 BC. However, The Bacchae and Iphigenia in Aulis were performed after his death in 405 BC and first prize was awarded posthumously. Altogether his plays won first prize only five times.

His plays, and those of Æschylus and Sophocles, indicate a difference in outlook between the three men, most easily explained as a generational gap, although with three great talents overlapping the driving forces may have pushed individual styles onwards perhaps faster than they may otherwise have done. Æschylus still looked back to the archaic period, Sophocles was in transition between periods, and Euripides was fully bonded with the new spirit of the classical age. When Euripides' plays are sequenced in time, they also show a developing pattern:

An early period of high tragedy (Medea, Hippolytus)
A patriotic period at the outset of the Peloponnesian War (Children of Hercules, Suppliants)
A middle period of disillusionment at the senselessness of war (Hecuba, Women of Troy)
An escapist period with a focus on romantic intrigue (Ion, Iphigenia in Tauris, Helen)
A final period of tragic despair (Orestes, Phoenician Women, Bacchae)

However, with over three quarters of his plays lost it is difficult to be certain as to whether the other works would also represent this development (e.g., Iphigenia at Aulis is dated with the 'despairing' Bacchae, yet it contains elements that became typical of New Comedy). In the Bacchae, he restores the chorus and messenger speech to their traditional role in the tragic plot, and the play appears to be the culmination of a regressive or archaizing tendency in his later works.

In one of his earliest surviving plays, Medea, includes a speech that he seems to have written in defence of himself as an intellectual ahead of his time, and to further challenge the times he has put the words in the mouth of the play's heroine:

"If you introduce new, intelligent ideas to fools, you will be thought frivolous, not intelligent. On the other hand, if you do get a reputation for surpassing those who are supposed to be intellectually sophisticated, you will seem to be a thorn in the city's flesh. This is what has happened to me."— Medea.

As we know Athenian tragedies during Euripides' lifetime were a public contest between playwrights. The state funded that contest and awarded prizes to the winners. The language was spoken and sung verse, the performance area included a circular floor or orchestra where the chorus could dance, a space for actors (usually three speaking actors in Euripides' time), a backdrop or skene and some special effects: an ekkyklema (used to bring the skene's "indoors" outdoors) and a mechane (used to lift actors in the air, as in deus ex machina). With the introduction of the third actor (an innovation attributed to Sophocles), acting also began to be regarded as a skill to be rewarded with prizes, requiring a long apprenticeship in the chorus. Euripides and other playwrights accordingly composed more and more arias for accomplished actors to sing and this tendency becomes more marked in his later plays: tragedy for him was a living and ever-changing genre.

Accounts by the famed comic poet, Aristophanes, characterise Euripides as a spokesman for destructive, new ideas, that mirror or help to bring about declining standards in both society and tragedy. However, 5th century tragedy was a social gathering for "carrying out quite publicly the maintenance and development of mental infrastructure" and it offered spectators a "platform for an utterly unique form of institutionalized discussion". A dramatist's role was not just to entertain but also to educate his fellow citizens—he was expected to have a message. Clearly this use of drama to democratize discussion was a very useful tool for all sides. Traditional myth provided the subject matter but the dramatist was meant to be innovative so as to sustain interest, which led to novel characterization of heroic figures and to use the mythical past to talk about present issues. The difference between Euripides and his older colleagues was, again, one of degree: his characters talked about the present more controversially and more pointedly than did those of Æschylus and Sophocles, sometimes even challenging the democratic order. Thus, for example, Odysseus is represented in Hecuba as "agile-minded, sweet-talking, demos-pleasing" i.e., a type of the war-time demagogues that were active in Athens during the Peloponnesian War. His concept is pleasingly simple. He retains the old stories and myths as well as the great names of the past and places them in the lives of contemporary Athenians thereby immediately help the audience understand it from the point of view of their own lives.

As mouthpieces for contemporary issues, they all seem to have had at least an elementary course in public speaking. Sometimes the dialogue often contrasts so strongly with the mythical and heroic setting, it looks as if Euripides aimed at parody, as for example in The Trojan Women, where the heroine's rationalized prayer provokes comment from Menelaus:

Hecuba:...O Zeus, whether you are the Law of Necessity in nature, or the Law of Reason in man, hear my prayers. You are everywhere, pursuing your noiseless path, ordering the affairs of mortals according to justice.

Menelaus: What's this? You are starting a new fashion in prayer.

Athenian citizens were familiar with rhetoric in the assembly and law courts, and some scholars believe that Euripides was more interested in his characters as speakers with cases to argue than as characters with lifelike personalities. They are self-conscious about speaking formally and their rhetoric is shown to be flawed, as if Euripides was exploring the problematical nature of language and communication: "For speech points in three different directions at once, to the speaker, to the person addressed, to the features in the world it describes, and each of these directions can be felt as skewed". Thus in the example above, Hecuba presents herself as a sophisticated intellectual describing a rationalised cosmos yet the speech is ill-matched to her audience, Menelaus (an unsophisticated listener), and soon it is found not to suit the cosmos either (her infant grandson is brutally murdered by the victorious Greeks).

Æschylus and Sophocles were innovative, but Euripides could move easily between tragic, comic, romantic and political effects, a versatility that appears in individual plays and also over the course of his career. Potential for comedy lay in his use of 'contemporary' characters, in his sophisticated tone, his relatively informal Greek, and his ingenious use of plots centered on motifs that later became standard, such as the 'recognition scene'. Other tragedians also used recognition scenes but they were heroic in emphasis, as in Æschylus's The Libation Bearers, which Euripides parodied with his mundane treatment of it in Electra (Euripides was unique among the tragedians in incorporating theatrical criticism in his plays). Traditional myth, with its exotic settings, heroic adventures and epic battles, offered potential for romantic melodrama as well as for political comments on a war theme, so that his plays are an extraordinary mix of elements. The Trojan Women for example is a powerfully disturbing play on the theme of war's horrors, apparently critical of Athenian imperialism (it was composed in the aftermath of the Melian massacre and during the preparations for the Sicilian Expedition) yet it features the comic exchange between Menelaus and Hecuba quoted above and the chorus considers Athens, the "blessed land of Theus", to be a desirable refuge—such complexity and ambiguity are typical both of his "patriotic" and "anti-war" plays.

Tragic poets in the 5th century competed against one another at the City Dionysia, each with a tetralogy consisting of three tragedies and a satyr-play. The few extant fragments of satyr-plays attributed to Æschylus and Sophocles indicate that these were a loosely structured, simple and jovial form of entertainment. However, in Cyclops (the only complete Euripides satyr-play that survives) the entertainment is structured more like a tragedy and introduced a note of critical irony typical of his other work. His genre-bending inventiveness is shown above all in Alcestis, a blend of tragic and satyric elements. This fourth play in his tetralogy for 438 BC (i.e., it occupied the position conventionally reserved for satyr-plays) is a "tragedy" that features Heracles as a satyric hero in conventional satyr-play scenes, involving an arrival, a banquet, a victory over an ogre (in this case, Death), a happy ending, a feast and a departure to new adventures.

Euripides was also a great lyric poet. In Medea, for example, he composed for his city, Athens, "the noblest of her songs of praise". His lyric skills however are not just confined to individual poems: "A play of Euripides is a musical whole....one song echoes motifs from the preceding song, while introducing new ones."

Much of his life and his whole career coincided with the struggle between Athens and Sparta for hegemony in Greece but he didn't live to see the final defeat of his city.

It is said that he died in Macedonia after being attacked by the Molossian hounds of King Archelaus and that his cenotaph near Piraeus was struck by lightning—signs of his unique powers, whether for good or ill. In an account by Plutarch, the complete failure of the Sicilian expedition led Athenians to trade renditions of Euripides' lyrics to their enemies in return for food and drink (Life of Nicias 29). Plutarch is the source also for the story that the victorious Spartan generals, having planned the demolition of Athens and the enslavement of its people, grew merciful after being entertained at a banquet by lyrics from Euripides' play Electra: "they felt that it would be a barbarous act to annihilate a city which produced such men" (Life of Lysander).

In The Frogs, composed after Euripides and Æschylus were both dead, Aristophanes imagines the god Dionysus venturing down to Hades in search of a good poet to bring back to Athens. After a debate between the two deceased bards, the god brings Æschylus back to life as more useful to Athens on account of his wisdom, rejecting Euripides as merely clever. Such comic 'evidence' suggests that Athenians admired Euripides even while they mistrusted his intellectualism, at least during the long war with Sparta.

Euripides had a famous library—one of the first to be privately collected. Although he lived most of his life in the midst of the cultured society of Athens, and was in some respects a leader in it, he grew bitter and despondent over the fierce rivalries and greedy ambitions which ran through the city. He loved the seclusion of his house at Salamis, where it was said that he composed his dramas in a cave.

Euripides fell out of favour with his fellow Athenian citizens and retired to the court of Archelaus, king of Macedon, who treated him with consideration and affection.

At his death, in around 406BC, he was mourned by the king, who, refusing the request of the Athenians that his remains be carried back to the Greek city, buried him with much splendor within his own dominions. His tomb was placed at the confluence of two streams, near Arethusa in Macedonia, and a cenotaph was built to his memory on the road from Athens towards the Piraeus.

Euripides – A Concise Bibliography

Alcestis (438 BC)
Medea (431 BC)
Heracleidae (c. 430 BC)
Hippolytus (428 BC)
Andromache (c. 425 BC)

Hecuba (c. 424 BC)
The Suppliants (c. 423 BC)
Electra (c. 420 BC)
Heracles (c. 416 BC)
The Trojan Women (c. 415 BC)
Iphigenia in Tauris (c. 414 BC)
Ion (c. 414 BC)
Helen (c. 412 BC)
Phoenician Women (c. 410 BC)
Orestes (c.408 BC)
Bacchae (405 BC)
Iphigenia at Aulis (405 BC)
Rhesus
Cyclops

Lost and Fragmentary Plays (Dated)

Peliades (455 BC)
Telephus (438 BC with Alcestis)
Alcmaeon in Psophis (438 BC with Alcestis)
Cretan Women (438 with Alcestis)
Cretans (c. 435 BC)
Philoctetes (431 BC with Medea)
Dictys (431 BC with Medea)
Theristai (satyr play, 431 BC with Medea)
Stheneboea (before 429 BC)
Bellerophon (c. 430 BC)
Cresphontes (ca. 425 BC)
Erechtheus (422 BC)
Phaethon (c. 420 BC)
Wise Melanippe (c. 420 BC)
Alexandros (415 BC with Trojan Women)
Palamedes (415 BC with Trojan Women)
Sisyphus (satyr play, 415 BC with Trojan Women)
Captive Melanippe (c. 412 BC)
Andromeda (412 BC with Helen)
Antiope (c. 410 BC)
Archelaus (c. 410 BC)
Hypsipyle (c. 410 BC)
Alcmaeon in Corinth (c. 405 BC) Won first prize as part of a trilogy with The Bacchae and Iphigenia in Aulis.

Lost and Fragmentary Plays (Not Dated)

Aegeus
Aeolus
Alcmene
Alope, or Cercyon
Antigone

Auge
Autolycus
Busiris
Cadmus
Chrysippus
Danae
Epeius
Eurystheus
Hippolytus Veiled
Ino
Ixion
Lamia
Licymnius
Meleager
Mysians
Oedipus
Oeneus
Oenomaus
Peirithous
Peleus
Phoenix
Phrixus
Pleisthenes
Polyidus
Protesilaus
Reapers
Rhadamanthys
Sciron
Scyrians
Syleus
Temenidae
Temenos
Tennes
Theseus
Thyestes

www.ingramcontent.com/pod-product-compliance
Lightning Source LLC
Chambersburg PA
CBHW060133050426
42448CB00010B/2094